W9-CGR-649

"This book deserves a broad audience. Everybody should read this book. In our businesses and our lives we all have communication failures that could easily be prevented with a little skill; but we are blind in the area. For example, I noticed in the 'Business of Listening' section that listening is tough for me as a broadcaster. There are simple things in this 80-page book for each of us—stories, tips and labs—that will greatly raise the effectiveness of our communication. Read this book—it's going to cost you next to nothing to read. You can substitute one evening of entertainment and make a difference in your life and work for years to come."
—Ali Velshi, Anchor, CNNfn

"In the 21st century, perhaps more than ever before, US soldiers need not only technical and fighting capability, but also leadership skills. The chief medium of leaders is communication. Zweifel's powerful yet simple principles, practices and tools enable leaders to use a free commodity – language – to produce breakthrough results."
—Col. Joseph LeBoeuf,
Head, Leadership Program, U.S. Military Academy, West Point

"This is the sort of book I love. Stimulating, inspirational, full of ideas you can use. I particularly like the weighting towards the importance of listening. It's the yin that most yang books on communication forget. Listening to understand others is one of the most empowering gifts we can offer. Enrich your own communication by reading this book."
—Peter Thompson,
Broadcaster and author of *Persuading Aristotle*,
Director, Centre for Leadership, Australia

"I keep this book with me at all times, I carry it in my briefcase, because you never know when you might need it to inspire a colleague, or brush up on your speaking and listening skills. An excellent book."
—Michael Gentz,
General Manager, ConocoPhillips Germany

"This is the first business book I have seen that emphasizes the importance of listening for producing results. Leaders must appreciate the other person's yearning to be understood. The book offers fascinating stories I had never heard in my five decades in the financial community, and that I could immediately relate my own experiences to. Communication is free, and it can transform reality. An outstanding, well-researched and extremely interesting book."

—Richard Murray,
Vice Chairman, LaProv Corporation

"*Communicate or Die: Getting Results Through Speaking and Listening* is a concise, wise and witty book that will help any company or team build its communication muscle—and increase its results exponentially while doing so. Nothing is more important or powerful than full communication—but research on the power of effective speaking and listening is rare, so Thomas Zweifel's book fills an important gap. Leaders and managers in any sector would do well to read this book and give it to their people."

—Lynne Twist,
President of The Turning Tide Coalition and
author of *The Soul of Money*

"Over the years, I have had the chance to teach generations of senior executives at Novartis in the art and science of leadership. I have seen all too often how senior managers or researchers in our industry can lose their credibility. Why? Because they talk, but they can't communicate in a way that produces high motivation. It really becomes an issue of *Communicate or Die.* This book is sorely needed for managers and teams who want to be leaders and make things happen."

— Guido Spichty,
Head, Novartis Leadership Program, Novartis AG, Switzerland

COMMUNICATE
OR DIE

Swiss Consulting Group Presents
The Global Leader Series™

COMMUNICATE OR DIE

Getting Results Through Speaking and Listening

THOMAS D. ZWEIFEL, Ph.D.

SelectBooks

Communicate or Die:
Getting Results Through Speaking and Listening
©2003 by Swiss Consulting Group, Inc.

First Edition

ISBN 1-59079-052-9

Library of Congress Cataloging-in-Publication Data

Zweifel, Thomas D., 1962–
Communicate or die : getting results through speaking and listening / by Thomas D. Zweifel.— 1st ed.
  p. cm. — (The global leader series)
Includes bibliographical references.
ISBN 1-59079-052-9 (pbk.)
1. Communication in organizations.
2. Interpersonal communication.
3. Listening.
4. Communication.
5. Miscommunication. I. Title. II. Series.
HD30.3.Z88 2002
658.4'5—dc21
                    2003004762

Manufactured in the United States of America
10 9 8 7 6 5 4 3 2 1

To Rani and the one million women in India
elected to panchayats (village governing councils)
in what is perhaps the greatest social experiment in history,
summoned to lead but not knowing how to lead;
who have to marshal more courage
and leadership every day
than you and I might summon in a year.

As for the best leaders, the people do not notice their existence.
The next best leaders, the people admire.
The next, the people fear, and the next the people hate.
But when the best leader's work is done,
the people say "we did it ourselves".

Lao Tzu, 6th century B.C.

Contents

Acknowledgments

I am grateful to so many people who directly or indirectly, knowingly or not, contributed to this book. Following are a few outstanding examples—

- Swiss Consulting Group's clients—including Aventis, Banana Republic, Citibank, GE Capital, General Motors, Goldman Sachs, JP Morgan, Lehman Brothers, Merrill Lynch, Nestlé, Novartis, Prudential, Siemens and UBS, as well as a host of small and medium-sized enterprises in the military, education and nongovernmental sectors—for using the knowledge and tools herein.

- Swiss Consulting Group's team and network of consultants worldwide, for constantly developing our body of knowledge and for contributing war stories to this book. In the United States, Tapas Sen, Dan Friel, Arthur Gutch, Richard Murray, Agnès Pégorier, Andrew Small, Peg Thatcher, Nick Wolfson and Yoram Wurmser. In Belgium, Sonia De Vos. In Brazil, Johannes van de Ven. In Canada, Jillian Cohen. In France, Poriya Vaudecrane. In Germany, Aurora Matticoli and Nirit Sommerfeld. In Switzerland, Tony Bächle. In Turkey, Sinan Arslaner. In Australia, Oskar Kamber. In Kenya, Uma Kakde. In the United Kingdom, Mick Crews. I love our work together.

- Robert Hargrove and my colleagues at Masterful Coaching for the opportunity to contribute to their clients.

- Joan Holmes and the global board and staff of The Hunger Project, for giving me access to a worldwide mission two decades ago.

- Deborah Gouge, for editing early drafts. Dave Ellis, for giving me advice on the business of writing and publishing. Anne Nelson, my first journalism teacher, for encouraging me to publish my writing. Vily Bergen, for seeing me as a fellow writer from the beginning. Julie Schwartzman, for being my toughest critic and best friend.

- Drs. Eva and Heinz Wicki-Schönberg, my parents, for being my first role models as global citizens.

Preface

Communicate or Die? That is quite a heavy-duty title. How can communication be a matter of life and death? Things can't be that terrible. After all, words are free, aren't they? Even babies know how to communicate to make sure they get what they need. So why should you bother reading a book on communication? Why not focus on the hard skills—strategy, finance, marketing or operations—that make a real difference?

Many of the toughest issues are caused—or at least compounded—by bad communication.

Two reasons. First, bad communication usually causes costly problems. Whether it is suicide bombers in the Middle East, where "everybody is always right," and nobody listens, as a friend tells me; or corporate accounting scandals; or a simple call to a large corporation that leaves you hanging in the labyrinth of its automated "customer service" voice menu (and when you finally get a live human being on the phone, you are asked to verify your account number and purpose of your call—even though you have just spent 10 minutes doing exactly that); many of the toughest issues are caused—or at least compounded—by bad communication. Companies go down, mergers fail, wars break out, families break up because people have stopped communicating.

Take just one story in the news: the question whether the FBI knew more than it now admits about the terrorists who struck the World Trade Center and the Pentagon on September 11, 2001. FBI agent and whistle-blower Coleen Rowley recently testified in a Senate Judiciary Committee hearing about the roadblocks to communication at the Bureau:

Communication is the biggest bang for the buck, the highest-leverage return on investment in any organization

We have a culture in the FBI that there's a certain pecking order, and it's pretty strong. And it's very rare that someone picks up the phone and calls a rank or two above themself. It would have to be only on the strongest reasons....If I say, "Why are we doing this, does this really have any value, does it serve a purpose?" it's either one of two things. It's just like a complaint; that we can all complain about it, but nothing can ever change, it just kind of falls on deaf ears and no one, like, really examines it. Or it might actually be seen, if you're criticizing some particular program write-up or some particular inspection thing, it actually might be seen as a challenge to somebody higher up and they may get mad or whatever.[1]

If the FBI had instituted a climate of open communication like the one at the organizations featured in this book, it would not have maneuvered itself into a quagmire. Who knows: it might even have performed better in fighting terrorism. Be that as it may—my experience with our clients tells me that the FBI is far from alone. It's no different in business, and the experience of whistle-blower Sherron Watkins at Enron was only the tip of the iceberg. Many managers or employees have to think very carefully before bypassing their direct superior. And if they speak up, they may do more harm than good, be it because they don't know how to make their case effectively or because many bosses are terrible at listening. This roadblock of course keeps vital intelligence or ideas from getting to the top, which in turn prevents innovation—or worse, leads to wrong decisions or wasted resources. Arguably, the DaimlerChrysler merger failed at the start not least because of sloppy communication. Daimler chairman Jürgen Schrempp never bothered to meet with the Chrysler people to tell them his expectations and to listen to theirs. The result: bickering, talent loss, brain drain, even lawsuits. When people cannot communicate effectively, things escalate, and you have to resort to divorce or war or the courts. The costs are enormous.

The second reason for *Communicate or Die* is my firm belief that, if properly harnessed and skillfully used, communication (yes, mere speaking and listening) is the biggest bang for the buck, the highest-leverage return on investment in any organization—for the simple reason that it is also one of the most under-researched and under-utilized levers for breakthrough results.

Communication costs next to nothing, yet it can resolve the most protracted issue and can literally save lives. Northern Ireland's breakthrough peace accord of 1998 has shown that effective communication can happen even after years and years of violence. Recently a group of Israelis and Palestinians met with negotiators of Northern Ireland's peace accord to learn how to jump-start communication. "Empowering your enemy will pay off for you in the end," David Grossman said afterwards. "If you only humiliate and delegitimize," the Israeli writer continued, "you will have nobody left to talk to."[2]

Similarly, as you will see in this small volume, companies from Abbott Laboratories to IBM have built their people's communication skills, thereby saving money and boosting productivity. I hope this book will make a contribution to your own ability to communicate, to shape reality and to cause results with your speaking and listening. Your life and work depend on it. So does, frankly, our common future.

TDZ, New York City, May 2003

Preface to
The Global Leader Series™

When I die I shall not be asked,
Why were you not Moses?
I shall be asked, Why were you not Zusya?
Rabbi Zusya quoted by Martin Buber[3]

Rani is an unlikely leader. From the lowly wash-ermen's caste, scorned by the Brahmin who have long dominated her village, she is illiterate, 30 years old and pregnant. But now Rani has been elected to the panchayat, the village gov-erning council, and she proclaims defiantly: "I am the boss."

India is largely a rural nation. There are some 500,000 villages with more than 600 million peo-ple—about one in every ten people on the plan-et. In the mid-1990s India passed a new law. Up to that time, for all of history, virtually all pan-chayat leaders had been men. But with the new law, one-third of all panchayat leaders must be women, which has led to the unprecedented fact

Many of these women leaders have powerful enemies. Alam Singh, a Brahmin farmer who used to rule Rani's village, said angrily: "She is stupid. She is illiterate. She doesn't listen to anybody."

that in every election one million women are elected to panchayat leadership positions. The problem is, these women have never known how to lead or manage, how to run an effective meeting, or how to make their voice heard. In fact, few of them ever lift their gaze above ground when they talk to someone. Many of them are Muslims and wear the customary veil that shields them from exposing themselves in public.

As if that were not enough of a challenge, many of these women leaders have powerful enemies. Alam Singh, a Brahmin farmer who used to rule Rani's village, said angrily: "She is stupid. She is illiterate. She doesn't listen to anybody." Another peer of Singh did not leave it at angry outbursts. When a woman in his village ran to unseat him as incumbent panchayat leader, he openly threatened to kill her if she won. She won. He carried out his threat and killed her. Then her daughter decided to run for her mother's seat, won it, and is still alive in office as of this writing.[4]

With the end of the Cold War, human issues that were long suppressed by ideology have become top priorities.

These courageous women stand for all people who are now summoned to lead, like it or not. As a result of the twentieth century and its revolutions, liberation struggles and waves of democracy, more and more people are now free to shape their own lives. The Internet and flattened organizational hierarchies allow each of us to make an impact on our organizations and societies. With the end of the Cold War, human issues that were long suppressed by ideology have become top priorities: children (at the 1990 Children Summit), sustainable development (1992 Rio Summit), population (1994 Cairo Summit), human rights (1995 Vienna Summit), social issues (1995 Copenhagen Summit) and women's rights (1996 Women's Summit in Beijing). In this new environment, we can no longer rely on our elected leaders to provide leadership alone. Each of us must lead—and we must be armed with the right tools for doing so. Leaders like Rani lead not from above but from below; they are co-creators, not autocrats.

The idea for this book came to me in 1996 when I prepared to leave my post as director of global operations at The Hunger Project after twelve years of service. The president of the organization asked me to write down in a "leadership manual" everything I had learned—principles, skills, methodology. On a lengthy and lonely drive home from a skiing trip, one hand on the steering wheel, the other clutching my Dictaphone, I spoke everything I knew about leadership into the little machine. I soon realized that if I were to do the assignment justice, it would take me years. So at that time I got away with writing a list. Now, half a decade later, after coaching dozens of entrepreneurs and Fortune 500 executives from Aventis to UBS, from GE Capital to GM, I can honestly say that The Hunger Project is the best organization I have ever seen at managing people—or rather, at generating leaders and empowering them to produce breakthrough results. And like Peter Drucker, I assert that all organizations, from firms to governments, from churches to the military, face essentially the same challenges. So it is time to make available the leadership secrets I have picked up from people like Nelson Mandela, but also from people like Rani. My clients have benefited from these secrets for five years; why shouldn't everybody else?

But aren't there enough books on the topic already? True, there are hundreds of books talking *about* leadership; there are memoirs of great leaders that tell inspiring stories about what they did in their time; there are the seven habits and the five golden rules and the ten spiritual laws or whatever; but in my view, few (if any) books give *access* to leadership. Now perhaps that is too much to ask of a book, which might simply tell a great story or give useful advice. But this book attempts to be different. What you are looking at is, as much as possible, a *workshop*. (And what workshops nowadays are available for a sub-$20 fee?) It comes fully equipped with tips, labs, even a trouble-shooting manual.

By the way, my last name "Zweifel" is the German word for "doubt" or "uncertainty" or "skepticism." It is ironic that someone named "Doubt" or "Doubting Thomas" would write a book on leadership, since leaders are supposed to be brimming with confidence. But perhaps the very essence of leadership is to doubt, to

> **If you want this book to be useful to you and your endeavor, you are going to have to go out into the action, into the market, into the battlefield, and actually live life.**

question, to be skeptical and not to accept things at face value. Maybe leadership is based on having doubts and acting nevertheless...much like the famous dictum by Arnold Schönberg, who reportedly said that courage is not the absence of fear, but action *with or despite fear.*

Speaking of doubts, let me saddle you with a few doubts right here. My first disclaimer: if you think that this book will make something happen, you are wrong. Books rarely accomplish anything; people do, and sometimes people accomplish things by reading a book. If you want this book to be useful to you and your endeavor, you are going to have to go out into the action, into the market, into the battlefield, and actually live life. This book—any book—can at best provide a framework for thinking before and between those actions. As my former teacher Adam Przeworski kept saying, "Theories are to be used, not believed." If you don't apply this book, it might be interesting, instructive, clever; but it will remain theoretical—it will not truly affect things.

This book works best if you approach it with a specific project, enterprise or relationship in mind. Take a few minutes right now and think of something that you really want—something that you cannot do by yourself, something that takes at least one other person to accomplish. Then say to yourself: "I will now use this book in such a way that I will get everything out of it that I can to achieve my goal."

Lab: Leadership-in-action

What objective is so vast that it would stretch you way beyond who you are today?

Better father, better husband, global mgmt position/career.

By when?

05/2007

What is missing in your leadership to meet this objective?

Self confidence, more efficient, determination life-balance, respect for others, understanding

---

What blockages (in you and around you) will you need to transcend to meet the objective?

- Communication skills, time constrains
- Cultural/Education aspects
- Family expectations to be certain way.

(I am aware that most people skip over these types of labs. But maybe you will find it in yourself to invest a few minutes in answering these questions. What would you want to get out of it to make it a worthwhile investment?)

My second disclaimer: there is not one universal, unified definition of leadership. Leadership has diverse connotations in different cultures, and most of them are misleading myths. In the American culture, the term leadership is used for just about anything that can be sold and that it makes sound better—from "leadership leases" to "leadership donors." Americans are often caught in the myth of "the faultless leader." We like to believe in

Camelot, the white knight who saves us from the mundane. If our leaders are not super-human in character, we discredit and soon discard them.

In our male-dominated culture that has prevailed for several thousand years, many people associate leadership with overbearing behavior, or with command and control. Nothing could be further from the truth.

In Germany and other German-speaking cultures, the word "leadership" would be translated as "Führerschaft"—not exactly a word you would want to use. Jewish scholars do

"Theories are to be used, not believed."

"not approve of lordship, because...no mortal can lord over another..." Rabbi Johanan reportedly said, "Woe to leadership, for it buries those who possess it."[5]

Even if there existed one unified definition of leadership, I would ask you to invent your own unique expression. As Martin Buber shows us in the motto at the head of this preface, your job is not to be like any other leader who came before you. That leader already did his or her job. Your job is to reveal your own life purpose and then fulfill that purpose with all your might.

A third disclaimer: your work with this book will be only as potent as your willingness to surrender to the coaching in the book. One basic ground rule for coaches is that we do not coach someone unless they are open to coaching. Even if it were possible to coach without a demand for coaching, the results would be limited or nil, and it would certainly not be fun. So whenever you ignore certain things that the book asks of you and you don't work things through, the integrated nature of the book will be lost, and you might not gain the benefits available.

Ask yourself whether you are willing to try the ideas in this book without nagging, judgment or evaluation. Can you simply do whatever the book asks you to do? After you have worked through the book, you will have complete free-dom to throw every one of them out. Try them on for now. Open yourself to the possibility that they might be useful to you.

One basic ground rule for coaches is that we do not coach someone unless they are open to coaching.

Did you know that typical politicians spend 90 percent of their time preventing others from unseating them, and only 10 percent working for the social good they have been elected to serve? Therefore, a final disclaimer: do not use this book for the wrong purposes. The book offers very powerful tools that can be used for building as well as destroying things or people. Leadership has already done much harm. Too many times, leaders have abused their power and caused damage. If you have any plans to continue this tradition, I ask you to give the book to someone else. As Gandhi said over 50 years ago, "Recall the face of the poorest and weakest man whom you may have seen, and ask yourself, if the step you contemplate is going to be of any use to him. Will he gain anything by it? Will it restore him to a control over his own life and destiny? In other words, will it lead to freedom for the hungry and spiritually starv-ing millions?" Will your undertaking uplift people in some way? Unless you have that intention, or at least unless that intention is part of your endeavor, you may want to rethink your enterprise before you continue.

Given that you are still reading, I will assume from now on that you and I both have positive intentions. As a working assumption, I believe that all people are driven to whatever they do either by love, fear or necessity. No matter what the motive, we can assume that people always have reasons—real or per-ceived—for their actions, and that they are trying to do the best they can under given circumstances. It is clear to me that such an assumption of best intentions is more often than not inaccurate, even naïve; but if I did not assume this, I would be unable to write this book. The question is this: at the end of your life, what will you say about your life? What will be written on your tombstone? Will you look back upon a life of going through the motions, or upon a life of meaning, service and contribution?

> Perhaps leadership is like fractals: the closer we look, the more confusing and the less defined leadership seems. Suppose someone asks you: How long is the coast of England?

Leadership is mysterious and unspeakable. Although I teach it at Columbia University, let me assure you: leadership is an art, not a science (but don't tell Columbia that). Perhaps leadership is akin to love: we know unequivocally whether it is present or absent, and yet it is hard to describe.

Or perhaps leadership is like fractals: the closer we look, the more confusing and the less defined leadership seems. Suppose someone asks you: How long is the coast of England? You might say 2,000 miles, and you would be close to accurate. But this answer is only true at a level of extraordinary simplification. The closer we come to the coast of England, the more we have to take into account all the circumferences of all the little pebbles. If we go even closer, we have to measure the circumferences of grains of sand. At the microscopic level, we are shocked to discover that the answer is that the coast of England is—infinite.

Despite—or maybe because of—all these paradoxes, I trust this book will provide you with concrete tools you can use in your own quest for leadership. And hopefully it will give you something else: the courage to live leadership on a daily basis—the courage to be Rani.

Chapter One

Non-Communication Can Kill

On the afternoon of March 23, 1999, Masaharu Nonaka, a manager at a Bridgestone affiliate in Tokyo, met with Bridgestone's president to complain about the company's restructuring policies. As the exchange grew more and more heated, Mr. Nonaka, whom Bridgestone officials knew as "normal," sincere and serious, became agitated. He suddenly stripped off his business suit to the waist, took out a pair of knives and screamed that he was going to commit hara-kiri. He stormed out of the meeting and slashed his stomach with a 14-inch fishing knife. Later that afternoon he died.

> That morning, Mr. Nonaka had sent a last, desperate e–mail message to all employees in his company. But management had erased the message before employees could read it.

That morning, Mr. Nonaka had sent a last, desperate e–mail message to all employees in his company. But management had erased the message before employees could read it.

Nonaka-san is probably the first corporate manager to commit the ancient Japanese ritual suicide because he and his company failed to communicate. His example is surely dramatic, but his problem hardly unique. We live in a different world today. Our time of massive mergers, rapid reengineering and unexpected dot-com crashes creates enormous tensions in the corporate workforce—tensions whose implications many managers fail to recognize.

First of all, Bridgestone is not alone, and hardly first, with its restructuring. In January 2001, DaimlerChrysler declared 26,000 job cuts, and the company's US car sales were projected to decline

1

The galloping market and its new prophets, the reengineering consultants and business strategists, are forcing a fundamental transformation onto managers and workers.

by 10 percent during that year. When Jürgen Dormann, the chairman of Aventis Hoechst, was asked whether his projected increases in turnover meant more jobs, he answered simply, "No." The surprised reporter followed up: "If not even in the high-tech pharmaceuticals industry, then where?" Dormann responded: "That's a good question. I don't participate anymore in the hypocrisy that blossoms everywhere. Our aim is to hold today's employment level. For that we must be extremely successful."[6]

But won't the new economy create jobs? It doesn't look like it. Dot-com layoffs rose by an astonishing 600 percent from July 2000 to January 2001. Former GE chairman Jack Welch would have made "significant" job cuts had the merger of GE and Honeywell ever come to pass: rumors spoke of 75,000 layoffs.

In January 2000, just days before DaimlerChrysler, the computer company Gateway announced 2,400 layoffs, and its president and CEO Jeffrey Weitzen admitted: "There is no way to sugarcoat the next several months." AOL–Time Warner announced a downsizing of 2,025 people; a day later Lucent said 10,000 would have to go. On a conference call, Hewlett-Packard's CEO Carly Fiorina told analysts grimly that the market was "like somebody turned the lights out."

These changes are hardly new, and some of the pressures they bring about have been present before. Already from 1989 through 1993, 1.8 million US workers lost their jobs in manufacturing, many of them due to the automation of their work.[7] In the mid-1990s, the Swiss-Swedish company Asea-Brown Boveri got rid of 50,000 people while increasing its turnover by 60 percent. The big banks and investment houses fire their 10 percent poorest performers even in the best of years, and "Neutron Jack" Welch got his name by streamlining General Electric even as things were going wonderfully. What *is* new is that the galloping market and its new prophets, the reengineering consultants and business strategists, are forcing a fundamental transformation onto managers and workers.

The New Great Transformation

Up to now, as part of the work contract, employers owed their employees a certain level of support. They helped finance their healthcare and pension, perhaps even their continuing education, and shielded them from the vagaries of the market. That is no longer the case. Impatient investors and boards demand streamlined operations that yield the highest possible margins and profits. Managers must minimize the use of expensive local labor by squeezing it in between technological rationalization and worldwide excess supply of cheap labor. Whether work steps are "outsourced" to self-employed contractors or sub-entrepreneurs, or whether external suppliers are integrated into the firm through joint ventures or M&As, it doesn't matter. The upshot for employees is that they are exposed like never before, in the old or the new economy. They face severe headwinds, from competition with their own peers, to cheap high-skill labor flooding in or telecommuting each day from Haiderabad or Johannesburg or Kiev.

The earlier capitalism was built on the exploitation of labor. The new capitalism is built on the exploitation of responsibility. In each organization, from General Electric to the hippest startup, responsibility is leveling out.

Welcome to the world of free agents. The ideal firm in this world would employ no labor whatsoever; it would only deal with entrepreneurs. It would be capitalism without workers. Everybody is an aspiring entrepreneur now. Everybody must unabashedly market and brand their services and themselves.

This is a transformation of capitalism itself. The earlier capitalism was built on the exploitation of labor. The new capitalism is built on the exploitation of responsibility. In each organization, from General Electric to the hippest startup, responsibility is leveling out. Whether you are a top manager or a front-line salesperson, you are held accountable for the performance of the firm and punishable by the market if you fail to perform. Before, colleagues helped to shape the work, now they must shape the business results. Before, they only had to participate and co-produce, now they must co-think and co-tremble day and night (and weekends). In 1979, the average white-collar manager worked 48 hour-weeks, five days a week. More recently, survivors report they work 70-hour weeks, six days a week.[8]

Newsweek reported in February 2001 that one of the top six fears of managers is that they might be jettisoned because they "don't have good leadership skills."

According to the new business philosophy, both sides enjoy greater profit from this new arrangement. It is supposed to be a win-win for both the giver and the taker, for the large and the small entrepreneur. Paradoxically, capitalism has become more democratic (though not more equal—far from it). We are all free to become dot-com billionaires, and we are all free to go under. In the brave new world of the employee-entrepreneur, "survival of the fittest" is the Darwinian metaphor for free, unfettered competition. To survive, managers and employees need to be leaders *and* enslave themselves; they need to calculate uncertainties; they need to risk their heads. Now everyone defines his economic fiefdom by acting as his own decentralized entrepreneur. Ambushed by the capitalist revolution, workers are driven into a market in which they can survive only as "free," agile and hungry actors— "leaders." *(Newsweek* reported in February 2001 that one of the top six fears of managers is that they might be jettisoned because they "don't have good leadership skills.")

What makes this inner-capitalist revolution particularly hard is that the main fault line is no longer between workers and capitalists. Much of the conflict is internalized now. The historical difference between capital and labor is transplanted, with all its potential gains and suffering, into the heart and head of the employee. Everyone must see themselves as their own capitalist and their own worker. The external opponent has disappeared from the social space and moved into the psyche of the individual.

Not long ago in San Francisco, a man jumped from the Golden Gate Bridge. He left a small note behind that said it all: "Survival of the fittest. Adios— unfit."

And whoever doesn't shape up will get some tough medicine. Two star authors among management consultants, Michael Hammer and James Champy, whose books on "reengineering of enterprises" sell in the millions worldwide, warn employers of too much leniency towards their workers, because it "would be a sign of weakness to only knock on their knuckles instead of breaking their legs."[9]

For some people, the stiff rules of what *Fortune* magazine has called the "new Darwinian workplace" are simply too much to bear. Not long ago in San Francisco, a man jumped from the Golden Gate Bridge. He left a small note behind that said it all: "Survival of the fittest. Adios—unfit."

Herding Cats: Leading Free Agents Under Uncertainty

Up to the latest downturn in the economy, being a free agent was cool. Cocky college students dreamed of being the next David Filo and becoming a dot-com billionaire in their 20s. They were arrogant and rash, and they could afford to be, so long as the gold rush lasted. After all, they might strike a vein of gold at any moment. Now they are not so sure. The first crack in the picture was the dot-com crash and disillusionment in 2000. Suddenly a mere great idea was no longer enough to get millions of dollars in venture capital. Now one had to demonstrate old-fashioned profitability to get money. Virtually overnight, venture capitalists stopped investing in new ventures unless they were predictably profitable. And the panic did not stop at the dot-coms: now there is clear evidence of a general economic downturn. Knowledge workers are still free agents, but fear has crept into the picture. Instead of billionaires, they might be bartenders tomorrow or collect unemployment.

How do you inspire middle managers and workers who are considering whether to leave your organization, and to open a bar, a surf school, a copy shop, a writing office or a limousine service?

Many others will simply say "enough" and get out of the rat-race of this new capitalism altogether. As protests in Seattle and Washington and Davos against the hegemony of global capitalism show, sizable numbers of people are unwilling to play the game of self-exploitation for self-profit. They forgo money in exchange for more time with their families and less stress; or they join nonprofits where they can make a difference and feel good about what they do. Recent studies estimate that 10–15 percent of the US population is "shifting down." The portion in European countries, whose social safety net permits people to collect unemployment while slowing down and smelling the roses, is likely even higher.

How do you lead people who feel fundamentally ill at ease in today's uncertainty? How do you inspire middle managers and workers who are considering whether to leave your organization in order to open a bar, a surf school, a copy shop, a writing office or a limousine service?[10] It lies in the nature of free agents that they go to the highest bidder. And the highest bidder might offer them values other than just money. You are not only fighting off your competitors, but all these bidders too.

How do you build loyalty in the age of free agents? How can you build and lead a team that will go into the trenches with you when they don't really have to? Can you be a leader who nourishes his or her team when the going gets tough? Can you find a way to empower the people who bring value to your organization? Those are the types of questions this book tries to answer.

Speaking not to employees, but only for the ears of investors, Pittman was enthusiastically unapologetic.

Bob Pittman, the former co-chief operating officer of AOL-Time Warner, seemed to have no intention of being a leader who empowered valuable people. For him it was not about people; it was simply about the need "to get the redundancies out," as he put it when he announced AOL-Time Warner's layoffs. Speaking not to employees, but only for the ears of investors, Pittman was enthusiastically unapologetic: "We are going to move at a pace that we think no other company of our size moves on. We are going to adopt 'quick, nimble, fast' as a corporate culture." Judging from his words, Pittman was far from the trenches where AOL's frontline people were fighting the company's battles for dominance. In fact, he seemed to care so little about his troops that if he ever went into the trenches, nobody would have followed him anyway.

Chapter Two

Communication Can Handle Anything

Now what does all this have to do with communication?

The connection is this: change causes upset. No, let me rephrase that. Change causes upset *in the absence of communication.* What is tragic about the hara-kiri at Bridgestone is that Nonaka-san would likely have survived had there been full and complete communication between him and his company's top managers. The bottom line: if you do not communicate effectively, you will lose your people. And even if they don't slash themselves with knives or jump off a bridge, you still lose their—

Change causes upset in the absence of communication.

and your—intellectual capital. It has become a truism of the knowledge economy that your company's most precious assets are no longer your machines, your inventory, your buildings. With few exceptions, your most precious assets are the people who can make the machines do great things. These employees are not just workers—they are carriers of intellectual property. They are "knowledge workers," as the management theorist Peter Drucker has called them: people who carry valuable intellectual assets in their heads. Some of their ideas are worth millions of dollars. In other words, your assets leave the plant or office every single night. If you cannot inspire them to come back in the morning—or if they come back only half-heartedly—you have lost the battle.

As if these challenges were not enough, several fault lines separate managers from free agents, administrators from knowledge

If you are in your forties, many of your knowledge workers are half your age.

workers, net-heads from sales people. A generational chasm is only one gap that makes communication difficult. If you are in your forties, many of your knowledge workers are half your age. They don't speak your language. They probably have not been brought up with your values. Geeks or not, they have grown up with laptops and e-mail and computer games. They are used to communicating with their machines, not with humans. They dance on the fine line between arrogance and ignorance. They have the world in front of them to conquer. They think they know everything. They probably don't like the Beatles, if they even remember them. They think you are boring, and they think you are *old*.

You thought that the dot-com crash and the old rules of profitability reined in their cockiness. "See what happens when you defy the laws of gravity? You fall on your nose. I told you so." But their attitude is unshakable. They are stuck on their old tricks just like you hold onto yours. And that does not bode well for team-building.

By contrast, if you are a manager in your 20s, how can you manage people double your age?

They have a point, too: the dot-com era may be over, but the Internet era has just begun. We are not at the beginning of the end. Quite the opposite: we are at the end of the beginning. The Internet is here to stay, and you better learn how to live with it. Leaders still need to lead in the connected economy.

By contrast, if you are a manager in your 20s, how can you manage people double your age? You just can't get how these old guys tick. What is their problem? Why are they so hung up about their families, their retirement or their golf game? Why are they so slow? Their methods are rigid, antiquated and predictable. What do they care about meeting agendas and protocol? Don't they know that good ideas are born when you sit on the can or take a shower, not in a dull meeting at the office? *Please*.

This generation gap is only one of many. Perhaps there are more than ever before in the globalized, diverse workplace: between men and women, African-Americans and Latinos, Americans and Pakistanis... and the list goes on.

Perhaps it has never been more difficult to lead, given all these differences and roadblocks: rapid change, uncertainty, globalization, diversity, competition, speed, a highly mobile workforce. But remember: leaders are not needed when things go well. Leaders are summoned in uncertain times, when the going gets tough, when things get out of hand. When it's smooth sailing, you can get by as a mere manager or even a caretaker, and pretty nicely at that. But when something is missing, when things are stuck, when there is chaos, you must lead. To use a football metaphor: leaders move

Leaders are summoned in uncertain times, when the going gets tough, when things get out of hand.

the ball down the field. Or if you prefer an artistic metaphor: "You have merely painted what is! Anyone can paint what is; the real secret is to paint what isn't," as the cantankerous sorcerer tells the lad Chi Po-shih, who is destined to become the greatest painter of 19th-century China.[11]

Why is communication so crucial to leadership? Because you cannot be a leader in isolation. A hermit in a cave or a monk meditating on a mountaintop needs no leadership skills. Your team will not implement even your best idea for a new application unless your communication is at least as compelling as the idea itself. To lead, you need to mobilize people; to mobilize people, you need strong relationships with them; and to relate powerfully, you need the skills and the ongoing commitment to communicate effectively. Communication is for leaders what water is for fish and air for birds. If you did nothing but live life as a quest to

be a great communicator—a great speaker *and* a great listener—
that quest in itself would make you a great leader.

The good news is that there are virtually no issues that cannot be resolved through communication. Effective communication can handle merger pains, problem accounts, employee
burnout, lawsuits, divorce and even war.

Effective communication can handle merger pains, problem accounts, employee burnout, lawsuits, divorce and even war.

The bad news is that most of us command a
small repertoire of communication skills. There
is precious little specificity in our speaking, and
almost none in how we listen to one another.
Before we examine specific distinctions of
speaking and listening, let's take a moment to
look at what communication can do for you.
Leaders go far beyond using communication
merely to acquire information ("Want fries with
that?") and to convey it ("Yes"). They use communication as a vehicle for generating action.
What the football coach says to his players in a huddle can shape
the play that results in a touchdown. Revolutionary leaders mobilize their troops through communication. In the 1940s, during the
Chinese revolution, Mao Tse-tung told his comrades that Chiang
Kai-Chek and his Kuomintang forces were an outwardly strong
but inwardly weak "paper tiger." This image of the paper tiger
became so real for Mao's followers that it gave them the confidence to bring about Communist victory in China. Steve Case and
his colleagues at AOL communicated the threat of Microsoft's
monopoly so vividly that it became a battle cry. They painted
Microsoft as a "dinosaur," a Tyrannosaurus Rex that would gobble
up everything in its way unless it was destroyed. (AOL's marketing
director, Jan Brandt, used even her car as a messenger in the war
against Microsoft: she changed her license plate from "2MILL," for
2 million AOL customers, to "FG8S"—for "F___ Gates.")

Few people have any idea how powerful their speaking and
listening can be. There is yet another function of communication:

we shape reality with our speaking and listening. I am not talking about *talking about reality.* I am saying that we create the world we live in—past, present and future—through language. If you say, "I don't trust him to be CEO," your words are not merely words; they create the reality of mistrust. Albert Einstein was well aware of how communication can shape reality when he said: "As a man speaks, not only is his

Few people have any idea how powerful their speaking and listening can be.

language in a state of birth, but also the very thing about which he is talking." By altering the way we communicate, we transform our reality. The philosopher Martin Heidegger knew this when he called language "the house of being":

> If it is true that man finds the proper abode of his existence in language—whether he is aware of it or not—then an experience we undergo with language will touch the inner-most nexus of our existence. We who speak language may thereupon become transformed by such experiences, from one day to the next or in the course of time.[12]

So language can transform us. And yet, "We don't realize how much we create reality through language," says Fernando Flores, founder of the consulting firm Business Design Associates, Inc. *Fast Company* magazine calls Flores a philosopher of language, so he should know. At twenty-nine, he was Chile's minister of economics—one of the youngest in any country—and in 1973 became minister of finance in Salvador Allende's democratically

We shape reality with our speaking and listening.

elected government. After the government was overthrown in a bloody military coup, Flores was jailed. His three years in prison provided him with crystal clarity on the power of communication. His words pierce through the fog around the issue. "If we say that life is hard, it will be hard. If, on the other hand, we make commitments to our colleagues to improve our productivity, we also improve our mood, and as a result, clarity and happiness will increase."[13]

Once you are aware of the power of communication and learn to harness it effectively, you see how people everywhere become victims of their own speaking and listening. You hear the CEO complain, "With these under-skilled people I can't get my job done." You hear the web developers grumble, "We don't have a prayer of getting this product to market." These descriptions of "reality" become self-fulfilling prophecies. In the vicious circle of language and life, language gives birth to life, life is reflected in language, and so on *ad infinitum.* "People talk about changing their thinking, but they have no idea what that is, let alone how to do it. The key is to stop producing interpretations that have no power," says Flores.

"People talk about changing their thinking, but they have no idea what that is, let alone how to do it. The key is to stop producing interpretations that have no power," says Flores.

Leaders cannot take communication with their team members for granted. They need to take words—theirs and other people's—seriously. When you take communication for granted, you pay a high price: you lose your ability to invent reality deliberately.

New technologies have opened up entirely new ways to communicate. Take only a few examples. More and more sales managers or tech consultants use Instant Messenger to ask their supervisors a question while they are on the phone with a client. David Ferris of Ferris Research, a market research firm in San Francisco, speculated that by 2005, the portion of business people using instant messaging would rise from about 5 percent to "about 60 percent of business users." Building managers in Manhattan use Internet-based software to manage luxury buildings, repair leaks in kitchen sinks and deliver packages even while tenants are traveling abroad. But new communication technologies reach far beyond business. Scientists working with the world's most powerful particle accelerator at the CERN physics laboratory near Geneva no longer have to travel there to conduct their experiments; instead, they can work together remotely, using the Grid Physics Network (GriPhyN) that offers vast computational power. Graduate students use their web-cams to keep their romantic relationships alive long-distance, from Beijing to San Francisco or from New York to Prague. In the Philippines, government soldiers and rebels of the Moro Islamic Liberation Front hurl insults at each other by texting them over their cell phones. Prison inmates in California and Arizona use the Internet to plead their cases, meet pen pals, or escape their feelings of solitary confinement. And a growing number of people now own Sony's Aibo ERS-210, a second-generation robotic dog, which, when outfitted with the proper software, will evolve from puppyhood to adulthood right before your eyes.[14]

> We simply send an e–mail so we don't have to listen. If we could produce our best results by just sitting alone at our computers, surfing, punching and clicking by ourselves, we would gladly do so.

But there is a pitfall for communication. We shop online, thumb our Blackberries or cell phones using ever-shorter acronyms, from LOL ("laughing out loud") to XLNT ("excellent"), from IMHO ("in my humble opinion") to RUOK? ("are you okay?"), but interact in real time only when absolutely necessary. We think our gadgets—our autoresponders, e–mail broadcasts and interactive Web sites—will do the communicating for us.

"Are we entering an era when you will never really touch or feel another human being?" asked peace activist John Wallach. "Will we use this new technology to become closer? Or farther apart?"[15] A recent study of workplace activity by the University of North Carolina in Chapel Hill found that so far, it is the latter: "rudeness and insensitivity toward others have proliferated to new heights of thoughtlessness." A majority of the study's 700 respondents blame this trend on the fragmentation of workplace relationships, facilitated by technologies such as voicemail, e–mail and teleconferencing. One manager said that "emerging technology takes away the human face—it's easy to 'flame' some-body you don't have to look at." Others said that work and information overload gives them less time for the polite "niceties" of business life.[16] After all, full and complete communication with another human being is a pain in the neck. It is hard work and risky—it might change us. Instead, we simply send an e–mail so we don't have to listen. If we could produce our best results by sitting alone at our computers, surf-ing, punching and clicking by ourselves, we would gladly do so.

While a former Microsoft hand insists that people are allowed to say No if they think a wrong decision is about to be made, others say that the company has become too big to listen to creative ideas.

But the worst thing you could do is to lean back and rely on the new technology to ensure communication. All that technology might sepa-rate us, and our humanity would go out the window. In the words of former secretary of state Madeleine Albright, "we remain far from mastering the art of human relations. We have invented no technology that will guide us to the destinations that matter most."[17] The paradox is, we are connected constantly, we surf on interactive websites, we have more e–mails from more people than ever before, but our interactive skills have likely suffered. What to do? The simple answer: tone your speaking and listening muscles. It's up to you to set the example by speaking produc-tively and listening masterfully.

Table 1 shows you the benefits of masterful listening and speaking, and the costs of failed communication. The horizontal X-axis goes from poor to great listening. The vertical Y-axis goes from poor to great speaking.

Four Quadrants of Communication for Results

GREAT SPEAKING but POOR LISTENING	GREAT SPEAKING and GREAT LISTENING
+ Focus.	+ Focus.
+ Good followers, good soldiers.	+ Breakthroughs.
– Potential leaders leave.	+ Speed.
– Results only where you have control.	+ High loyalty: workers do whatever it takes.
– No self-generating leadership.	+ Straight talk, "hard love."
– Little innovation.	+ Sustainable leadership culture: only leaders.
POOR SPEAKING and POOR LISTENING	POOR SPEAKING and GREAT LISTENING
– Slow death.	+ Innovation.
– Isolation, fragmentation.	+ Self-expressed employees.
– Misunderstandings, conflict.	– Lack of focus.
– Missed opportunities.	– Waste of time and money.
– Burnout. High employee turnover.	– Management by committee.
– Low trust level. Lawsuits.	– Anything goes.
– Post-merger pains.	

Table 1. The four quadrants of communication for results. X-axis = poor to great listening; Y-axis = poor to great speaking.

In the southwest quadrant—where leaders are poor speakers and poor listeners—organizations experience slow death: people's work is isolated or fragmented, they misunderstand each other, conflicts are frequent, opportunities fall through the cracks. Employees burn out quickly and leave because they feel little loyalty. They might even resort to lawsuits because they don't trust their leaders and have given up on even the possibility of communication. One example for this quadrant at the moment is DaimlerChrysler, whose head Jürgen Schrempp has demonstrated careless speaking combined with poor listening to other viewpoints. DaimlerChrysler's severe post-merger pains, including lawsuits and resignations of executives, are in large part due to

While FDR used radio skillfully to shape the attitudes of millions of his followers with his "fireside chats," we know from accounts by Generals George Marshall and Joe Stillwell that he was a poor listener by today's standards.

poor speaking and poor listening. (Of course the company might move out of this quadrant quickly. Besides, poor communication is not the only issue DaimlerChrysler faces. Another is of course the cyclical and volatile automobile market. One post-merger issue, the lack of cultural integration, is the focus of the next chapter.)

Organizations in the northwest quadrant, skillful speaking but poor listening, typically have great focus and a workforce that stands united behind their leader (usually one very charismatic leader). Intel and its leader Andy Grove, and Microsoft and its leader and "chief software architect" Bill Gates are examples of this quadrant. While a former Microsoft hand insists that people are allowed to say "no" if they think a wrong decision is about to be made, others say that the company has become too big to listen to creative ideas. There are all sorts of bureaucratic hurdles to overcome, starting with the need to prove to Gates and CEO Steve Ballmer that your new idea will mesh with Microsoft's strategy. "It just got so frustrating," says Eric Engstrom, an eight-year Microsoft veteran who left Microsoft in the late 1990s to co-found Chromium Communications. "You want to do innovative work, but you have to spend half your time defending your turf."[18] (Later in their careers, both Gates and Grove recognized the need to improve their communication skills—specifically the need to match their powerful speaking with equally powerful listening.)

In the political sphere, Franklin D. Roosevelt is a prime example for the great speaking/poor listening quadrant. While he used radio skillfully to shape the attitudes of millions of his followers with his "fireside chats," we know from accounts by Generals George Marshall and Joe Stilwell that FDR was a poor listener by today's standards. Stilwell especially noted his frustration over presenting detailed reports to the President, only to have them fall on deaf ears.[19]

The southeast quadrant shows the opposite: the leader speaks poorly but listens skillfully. Examples in this category are hard to find, and that is not by accident. The media is biased toward speech and rarely covers leaders who listen masterfully but speak poorly. After all, we have *talk shows.* Ever heard of a Sunday morning *listening show?* One example is the head of one of our client companies, whose great listening skills are not matched by his speaking. The result is that while there is innovation, and while employees feel they have a voice in shaping its future, the company lacks focus and direction.

Jack Welch at GE is known for listening carefully for best practices in every meeting.

Finally, leaders in the northeast quadrant combine great speaking with great listening—and the results show it. Organizations in this quadrant do not depend on a single leader; rather, leadership is embedded in the organizational culture. Nokia is an example for this category. During the annual "Nokia Way," management takes input from all employees worldwide in shaping its strategy each year. CEO Jorma Olilla and his peers at the Helsinki head office integrate that input and communicate it powerfully around the world. The result is that middle managers speak passionately about Nokia's strategy—without first having to search their files for a mission statement. Another example is Jack Welch at GE, who is known for listening carefully for best practices in every meeting. Acting as a membrane, he communicates these new ideas immediately to GE offices around the world. Welch continually reshapes GE with what he has heard. Also, he reportedly follows up in writing on every point raised by anyone in his meetings. So does Larry Bossidy, the chairman and CEO of AlliedSignal.

A nonprofit example is The Hunger Project, whose leader Joan Holmes is a compelling speaker who mobilizes thousands of

Only through skillful and compelling speaking and listening was King able to alter the course of history.

activists with her speeches, but who has made listening a policy essential to fulfilling the organization's mission. When The Hunger Project launches its work in a country, it does not come to tell people what to do. It comes to listen. And it listens to hungry people not as a problem but as the solution, as the key change agents in ending hunger.

A final example in the great speaking/great listening category is Martin Luther King, a transcendent leader guided by the "dream" of racial equality. King dreamed his dream because he listened to thousands upon thousands of his contemporaries in hundreds of churches and rallies across America. He listened not only to his yes-men, but also to opposing points of view—and much to the frustration of his aides, all night if necessary. He then spoke his dream—really an amalgamation of all the dreams he had heard—to millions of people in the most stirring words. His speaking gave his listeners a voice. Only through skillful and compelling speaking *and* listening was King able to alter the course of history.

Gandhi had to unleash the second-largest population in the world with scarcely more than the means of radio (and, believe it or not, a slight speech defect).

By the way, today's leaders can learn a lot from leaders like King or Gandhi or Mandela, each of whom was forced to lead an entire movement remotely. King was in and out of jail and often had to guide his movement from prison; so did Mandela, who was imprisoned on Robben Island for 27 years. Gandhi had to unleash the second-largest population in the world with scarcely more than the means of radio (and, believe it or not, a slight speech defect). In that sense, each of them might well have been a global leadership pioneer.

But of course Gandhi, King and Mandela worked without fax and e-mail, PCs, cell phones and pagers. The landscape in which we communicate has changed, and leaders must be aware of the implications. When you pop someone an e-mail message, your communication is stripped of the stuff that you rely on to help you get your point across. You can't use your appearance, gestures, body language, your expressions, tone of voice or even your handwriting. In the virtual environment, communication is reduced to its bare bones—listening and speaking. Even in a Webcast or a videoconference where participants see each other, you cannot rely on the immediacy and easy informality that exist when speaker and listener are in the same room. The same joke or aside that causes a laugh across the table can ruffle a listener's feathers when you communicate across cyberspace.

When you pop someone an e–mail message, your communication is stripped of the stuff that you rely on to help you get your point across.

In the rest of this chapter, we explore distinctions in both speaking and listening that will enable you to deepen your communication effectiveness in any medium—meetings, conference calls, press briefings, e–mail broadcasts— virtual or real-time. You can communicate in a way that sabotages the future, or in a way that enhances it. The more effective you are as a communicator, the more powerful you are at producing the results you want—a hallmark of effective leadership.

Where Exactly Is Your Communication?

One of the things you should recognize off the bat is the domain of your communication. Look at Figure 1. Communication falls into four domains that usually, but not always, build on each other. Do stockbroker types call you, too? They call me on the phone and say: "Hey Tom, I got this great portfolio that would be perfect for you. You will love this offer." This is a typical action-communication when there is no relationship, no vision, no planning whatsoever. The result is that I simply wish them a good day and hang up the phone.

Communication for Results Pyramid™

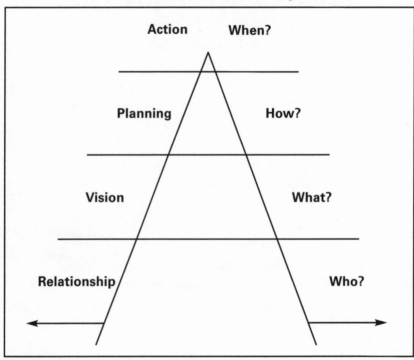

Figure 1: The Communication for Results Pyramid™. The broader your foundation of relationship, the higher you can build.

On the ground floor of **relationship**, you answer the question, "Who are we?" To build relationship, you have to be genuinely interested in the other person: who are they? Where do they come from (and I don't just mean their birthplace)? What are their values? What makes them tick? The ground rule is that the deeper the foundation of your relationships, the higher you can build the pyramid of accomplishment. Without at least some basic trust, you cannot build a meaningful accomplishment—a point easily lost on most of the Western world in which the court system has largely replaced a system of trust based on relationship.

Once you have built a solid partnership, the second floor is **vision**. Here you answer the questions, "What are we here for? What is possible? What do we want to accomplish?" Communications to create vision should avoid censorship or evaluation or skepticism (they belong to the next floor). Pretty much anything is possible at this stage. It is here that you ask people, and yourself, to think outside the box—to dream.

> When your communication partner is upset, you can be pretty sure that relationship is missing. Rather than charging full-speed ahead, it is a good idea to go back to strengthening the ground floor of relationship.

Standing on the foundation of relationship, and inspired by a common vision, you can now move into the realm of **strategy**. Here you ask: "How do we get it done?" This is where all the skeptics and nay-sayers should come in and ask tough questions. This is where you think your

accomplishment through to the end: budgets, timelines, who does what when, what could go wrong, details that might fall through the cracks, what comes after the project, and so on.

Only when the planning is complete and your team is clear on the 'How,' it is time to move into **action**. Here is where you make commitments and requests, and every word you say is geared toward catalyzing action.

Of course, communication does not always happen in the linear fashion suggested by Figure 1. It is quite possible to create a powerful partnership that allows you to jump straight into action. It is even possible to start an interaction with someone you don't even know by requesting an action right away, but I don't recommend it—unless you are one of those desperate stockbrokers...In general, it is unwise to skip a floor before you move on to the next one.

Imagine that each of the floors of accomplishment has its own built-in alarm. When your communication partner is upset, you can be pretty sure that relationship is missing. Rather than charging full-speed ahead, it is a good idea to go back to strengthening the ground floor of relationship.

The bottom line is that you should always distinguish in which domain you are communicating, and adjust your communication to that domain.

When people are resigned to the past, what is missing is a common vision. So when you pick up signs of resignation around you, you want to rekindle the vision that brought you all together in the first place.

When people are unsure what to do, or when they move too slowly, the strategy and tactics are probably unclear to them. In that case, they don't need to be yelled at. What they do need is a better sense of how to go about achieving the vision, so your communication needs to focus on the How until you can be sure that they have a clear pathway for action. At this stage, you want to ask questions like, "What is missing for you to deliver on our vision? What are the obstacles? What could go wrong, and how can we prevent that? What are your immediate opportunities?"

Finally, when people don't keep their agreements or don't take the actions needed, a communication for action is missing— if, and only if, the other three floors have been built. If people don't come to your meeting on time, it is not necessarily because they are sloppy or forgetful. Perhaps they are late because they don't experience partnership with you, they don't feel like stakeholders, they don't own your vision, they can't see the way through, or they need a better visual display of their commitments and agreements that pulls for the right actions and practices.

The bottom line is that you should always distinguish in which domain you are communicating and adjust your communication to that domain. Each of the four floors has its own do's and don't's. Try to distinguish each speaker's intention: on which floor of the pyramid are they? Are they attempting to deepen their relationship with you or your enterprise? Are they envisioning a new possibility? Are they posing an opportunity that requires some planning and thinking through? Or are they offering or demanding specific action? Most people have no idea of the domain in which they are communicating. Just by making these distinctions, your communications are likely to make a leap in effectiveness. At the very least, you will avoid misunderstandings and wasteful or inefficient talk.

Unless your company culture is used to studying written memoranda, it probably won't make any difference to send out another lengthy, highly technical e–mail broadcast in 8-point font about strategy.

But choose your medium wisely on any floor of the pyramid. Unless your company culture is used to studying written memoranda, it probably won't make any difference to send out another lengthy, highly technical e–mail broadcast in 8-point font about strategy. Nobody will get back to you. Nobody will ask you about your memo because none of your team members wants to be seen as stupid. So they simply ignore your e–mail. People will shrug and hit the Delete button. A better call might be to have a meeting with some key people where you explain the strategy and leave ample room for Q&A. That way you'll be sure the strategy sticks.

Marshall McLuhan's slogan is still an ironclad rule in the digital age: "The medium is the message." You know already not to use e–mail but the phone or a dinner to build a new relationship. You can sustain relationships by e–mail, but it's almost impossible to build one unless you are both in real time. Beyond that, be clear on the organization's communication culture, and choose the medium that will get the job done. If the organizational culture is meeting-happy, then you need to hold a meeting to build alignment on your vision. If the culture is not one of oral but of written communication, don't call people on the phone unless you have to, but communicate in memos and e–mails, and write well in advance of your desired decision so the recipients have time to consider your communication. No matter what you do, stand in the shoes of the recipient and use the medium that makes it easiest for the recipient to get your communication. In sum, make your communication user-friendly.

Now that we have distinguished the four floors of communication for results, we look at the first aspect of communication— the crucial but virtually invisible aspect of listening. Before you even open your mouth, make sure you build and tone your listening muscles.

Chapter Three

Leading by Listening

Listen! Or your tongue will make you deaf.
Cherokee saying

America Online was losing customers in droves.

The problem was not that the company was failing to win new customers. Quite the contrary: during the March 1996 quarter, 905,000 new "members" had signed on—a record. AOL had passed the astonishing milestone of five million customers, and its 1996 goal was the magic 10 million mark. But something was wrong. AOL executives called it the "churn" factor: more and more customers were dropping out, and the number of dropouts—an average of 6 percent a month—rapidly approached the

Finally, Steve Case had an idea. In all the marketing and strategizing activity, the company had not really listened to its customers.

number of the new ones. The legendary growth in AOL members was coming to a screeching halt. And all the marketing and advertising gimmicks, all the free disks that AOL sent to millions of households, all the features the firm added to its service, all the long internal strategy meetings—nothing helped.

Finally, Steve Case had an idea. In all the marketing and strategizing activity, the company had not really listened to its customers. Case appointed Audrey Weil as head of member experience. Weil traveled to AOL's Jacksonville call center in the summer of 1996 to listen and see what its members wanted and why they were dropping out.

Listening is one of the best-kept secrets of effective leadership.

Here is what she found. Many AOL members were frustrated by the ticking clock. They felt duped, since the company stubbornly refused to change from expensive per-hour rates to what had become the ISP industry standard—unlimited online time for $19.95 a month. When, on top of that, members were unable to get online because AOL's capacity was stretched beyond its limits, they got angry. Many of them simply left in frustration.[20] This customer mutiny happened because AOL was not listening.

Listening is one of the best-kept secrets of effective leadership. By sending Weil to listen to AOL customers, Case showed that he understood the fundamental link between listening and leadership: when we speak, we learn very little, because we merely say what we know already. When we listen, we may learn something new, while bestowing on others the gift of our attention. Former US Secretary of State Henry Kissinger illustrates this connection between listening and learning. Gore Vidal writes about meeting him in Rome:

> Although Kissinger and I were careful to keep some distance apart, I could hear the ceaseless rumbling voice in every corner of the chapel. The German accent is more pronounced in Europe than on television at home. He has a brother who came to America when he did. Recently, the brother was asked why he had no German accent but Henry did. "Because," said the brother, "Henry never listens."[21]

Already Socrates understood the connection between listening and learning: students at his school in ancient Athens were forbidden to talk during their entire first year of study. And the listening-learning linkage is far from trivial for business. Imagine a company with seven reporting levels. If the people at every level report 50 percent of what they know up to the next higher level—and 50 percent is a rather optimistic number—the leader at the top will know less than 2 percent of what is actually going on. If control resides solely at the top, the consequences of being that out of touch can be disastrous for decision-making. Imagine what happens if the leader happens to base his or her decisions on the 98-plus percent of wrong information. In today's complex and fast-changing organizations, chief executives depend on vital strategic information from others, both within the organization and from outside it. Listening is a crucial vehicle for getting that strategic intelligence.

Although listening is a fundamental skill, we are not taught how to do it. There are very few how-to books and virtually no schools on listening skills.

Yet listening is an undervalued commodity. One chief executive, reminded of the importance of two-way communication, snapped: *"Of course I use two-way communication! I communicate to my people both verbally and in writing!"*

Unfortunately, this executive is not alone. Nobody seems to listen anymore. Instead, talk abounds in our society. Day and night, we are inundated with infomercials and e-mail broadcasts urging us to buy this or try that. It seems that everyone has something to say. Oftentimes, when people tell others to "listen," what they really mean is "shut up" so they can talk. Especially in the Western culture, the important people talk, while those who have nothing to say listen. Listening is so invisible that it goes virtually unrecognized. Listening makes no noise, is intangible, and leaves little evidence, while talk is loud, gets attention, and can be recorded.

Although listening is a fundamental skill, we are not taught how to do it. There are very few how-to books and virtually no

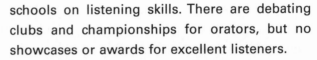

I have seen people's initiative crushed, performance break down, or mergers go awry—all because of poor communication and listening skills.

schools on listening skills. There are debating clubs and championships for orators, but no showcases or awards for excellent listeners.

Most people have a mechanistic, black-and-white understanding of listening. At best they treat listening like a light switch to turn on and off, and fail to see the rich body of distinctions listening can be. But much like painting or strategy, listening is a complex art—one that takes sustained effort to develop, but yields surprising results to those who dare to make it a life-long quest.

Listening produces real effects. You can make or break people by the way you listen to them. When Oprah Winfrey listens to guests on her show, she—or more precisely, her empathy—turns ordinary people into fascinating human beings. Winfrey says that her emotional connection to her guests is a way of relating to people that grew when she was a television news reporter. She explains, "You're at a plane crash and you're smelling the charred bodies, and people are coming to find out if their relatives are in the crash and they're weeping, and you weep too because it's a tragic thing."[22] The same empathetic listening that made Winfrey cry while reporting the news made her an instant success as a talk-show host and one of the wealthiest and most powerful media leaders.

Just as listening to others can embolden and enable them, not listening can damage a person's spirit and effectiveness. I have seen people's initiative crushed, performance break down, or mergers go awry, all because of poor communication and listening skills. In a survey of 22,000 shift workers in various US industries, 70 percent stated that they have little communication with plant and company management, and 59 percent said that their companies do not care about them—which is another way of saying that nobody listens to them.[23]

> **Tip.** Consider for a moment that all the people you know—every one of them, without exception—show up the way they do as a function of how you listen to them. Assuming that this is true, what would it mean about your power to create reality?

Not everyone is deaf to the importance of listening. There are businesses that recognize listening as essential to effective management—"A good boss knows how to listen," in the words of Kurt Abrahamson, group president at Jupiter Media Matrix.[24] After IBM–Canada's stock fell and the company had to lay off 5,000 of its 13,000 workers in the mid-1990s, management realized that IBM, much like AOL, had to listen to its customers. The company made customer relationships a top priority. The result: IBM-Canada accomplished a major turnaround. By 1998, its workforce was back to over 13,000 people.[25] Abbott Laboratories' sales techniques turned off customers until the company implemented a program to mend customer relationships and improve employees' listening skills through targeted training. As a result, 200 problem accounts improved between 1995 and 1997, resulting in $9 million in additional sales.[26] Another business that recognizes the value of listening is HPM, an American die-casting company. Chief Executive Neil Kadisha explains his policy of listening to his employees:

> No one has a thing to fear about coming to me and lodging a complaint or making a suggestion. In all of my companies, janitors to the highest level of management can come to me.... We manage by respect, not by fear. We respect our employees' opinions and suggestions. They have the right to get upset and angry, and they have the right to be heard.[27]

These companies and others are serious about the need to listen. They have incorporated listening into their business practices, often with significant improvements in performance and efficiency.

How is it possible that a person's performance and effectiveness could improve simply as a result of how you listen to that

The bottom line: listening is the smartest investment I know.

person? That question is best answered by another: Can you recall a time when you felt completely heard and understood by another human being? Most of us have had that experience. We probably all remember rare moments when, regardless of what we said, our words were brilliant because they meant something to someone. In *The Lost Art of Listening,* Michael P. Nichols explains why we crave those moments: "Few motives in human experience are as powerful as the yearning to be understood....Being listened to means that we are taken seriously, that our ideas and feelings are known and, ultimately, that what we have to say matters."[28] When your team members are taken seriously, they perform just as seriously. When someone treats you as though your words matter, you function as though your performance matters.

Tip. If you want to generate accomplishment and excellence around you, become a masterful listener. Few things you can do as a leader yield higher leverage.

The bottom line: listening is the smartest investment I know. It's free (well, almost free—I guess there are some opportunity costs), and if you listen well, you generate valuable intellectual property. Listen to fresh views, and you'll get new ideas and innovation. Listen to frontline people that are in touch with the market, and you get market analysis. Listen carefully, and you reveal what is missing for success. You may uncover blind spots you didn't know existed before.

The Chinese word for *listening* also means *eyes, ears, you, undivided attention* and *love.* The practice of listening consistent with these rich meanings may well be one of the most important leverage points in shaping your company's future. To say it bluntly: shut up and listen for a change. Amazing things might happen.

Climb the "Matterhorn of Masterful Listening"

We have seen above that listening is far from a "soft" skill. Both listening and failing to listen have hard consequences. Those who do build their listening muscle gain direct access to accomplishment. As your mastery of listening grows, you expand exponentially the reach of what you can accomplish. Figure 2 illustrates the "Matterhorn of Listening and Results" that ranges from Ignoring—no listening whatsoever—to Generating—complete listening that generates the speaker's brilliance and leadership. The peak of the Matterhorn represents mastery: the ability to listen to other people's listening while you are speaking. The size of your accomplishment grows exponentially along this continuum. As you and your team climb up towards the peak of Mastery, your listening strengthens

The "Matterhorn of Masterful Listening" ranges from Ignoring— no listening whatsoever— to Generating— complete listening that generates the speaker's brilliance and leadership.

the team, catalyzes innovation and produces leaps in productivity. We now look more closely at each level.

Level Zero: Ignoring

Shortly before the 1979 revolution in Iran, a *New York Times* reporter interviewed Ayatollah Ruhollah Khomeini in Paris. "He didn't like any of my questions," she recalled two decades later. "So he simply stood up from his cross-legged position on the floor and, without a word, wrapped himself in his cloak and left the room." Khomeini's biographer agreed with the journalist: "Khomeini had never been particularly interested in dialogue," he writes. "He was an introvert; his dialogue was with himself rather than with others.[29]

Ignoring is simply the absence of listening. It's ground zero. You ignore a communication by dismissing it. Ignoring includes interrupting the speaker, fidgeting with paper or pencil—or your mouse—as someone speaks to you, or crowding out the speaker's words by the force of your internal chatter. As in the example with Khomeini, ignoring is often a way to exert power over someone, wittingly or unwittingly. If a newcomer presents a new idea in the monthly meeting, all too often she is simply dismissed.

The Matterhorn of Masterful Listening

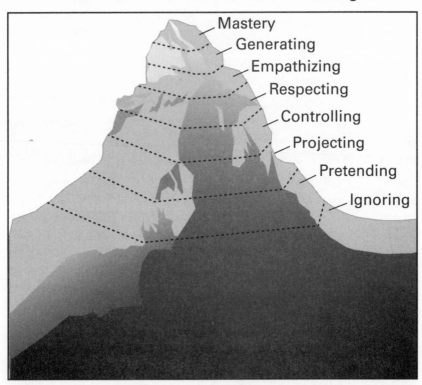

Figure 2. The "Matterhorn of Masterful Listening." Your results increase exponentially with the quality of your listening.

Ignoring someone is more than merely rude or passive-aggressive. It can have far-reaching effects. When a mathematics professor at a small Virginia college politely called an Intel technical support operator to report that the company's Pentium chip had miscalculated a complex division problem, the company ignored him. The professor did not remain polite for long. He disseminated his complaint on the Internet, and soon the issue blew up into what CEO Andy Grove has called the worst time in his career: "I felt we were under siege—under unrelenting bombardment."[30] Finally, after a public outcry, Grove and Intel's management came around to listening. Intel offered to replace the processors

When a college professor called Intel support to report that the company's Pentium chip had miscalculated a division problem, the company ignored him. The professor did not remain polite for long.

of all users who wanted them replaced for whatever reason. In addition, Grove ordered the creation of a consumer-complaints division to listen to Intel customers and take their complaints seriously. "We had not been in the consumer business in any big way before, so dealing with consumer questions was not something we had ever had to do," Grove explained. "Now, suddenly, we did from one day to another and on a fairly major scale." Intel had learned its lesson about the importance of listening the hard way.

The philosopher Martin Buber illuminates in his seminal book *I and Thou* why ignoring someone can be so damaging. Buber argues that you and I exist only in relation to each other. If relationship is the source of our existence, and if relationships are sustained and deepened through communication, then communication is the medium for our existence. It is through communication between you and your colleagues that they cease to be objects and that you influence, shape and mold each other. By the same token, your ignoring them denies their existence. It takes away their humanity and condemns them to being mere things that can be managed— shuffled around, outsourced, made redundant or manipulated.

Most women cannot even count the times and ways their communications were ignored.

Most women cannot even count the times and ways their communications were ignored. (The same is true for many minorities.) Aboubacar Kourouma, director of The Hunger Project-Senegal, confesses, "One of the first things I've had to learn to do in this job is listen to women." Unlike Kissinger (at least if we are to believe his brother), Kourouma learned his lesson: "When you listen, you learn a lot. We learn how to do our work." Unfortunately, many managers have not yet learned that lesson. Women in much of the world have internalized that they have no voice. In China, for instance, when a woman is alone in the house and someone knocks or rings the bell, it is not uncommon for her to reply, "Nobody is home." She has been ignored so long that she now ignores herself. Ignoring may be the ultimate weapon of dehumanizing a person.

Ignoring is rampant in organizations and produces real opportunity costs, not to speak of a massive waste of energy. Nonaka-san's hara-kiri suicide is only the tip of the iceberg. Few things damage a company more and faster than when its stakeholders ignore each other's communications. One person makes a request of another, who accepts and then ignores the request purposely or unwittingly. I see this happen on a weekly basis. When the CEO of a client urgently requested that a senior manager contact a competitor that had just gone bankrupt to offer assistance in servicing its pending jobs, his communication simply fell through the cracks because it lay outside business as usual. Ignoring his request cost the company as much as $500,000 in lost revenue. Worse, ignoring requests plunges people into resignation and weakens the power of future commitments and requests ("He never really means it anyway" or "Here we go again"). When I come across organizational breakdowns, a frequent root cause is simply that people ignore each other's communications. This root cause itself is often ignored. Surprise.

> **Tip.** The more you try to ignore something, the more energy it takes to keep ignoring it. Notice what happens if you tell yourself not to stare at a blemish on someone's face. Still ignoring it? Good! Now ignore that you are ignoring it...

Level One: Pretending

During the weekly staff meeting at Handango, a Texas software startup, marketing executive Wendy Gibson was typing an urgent message to an intern on her two-way pager—BLT, hold the mayo.

Meanwhile, James Lowe, in charge of business development, was booking hotels and checking flights for his vacation to China—on his wireless Palm. Will Pinnell, a developer, was trying to entice any Palm-wielding colleague within infrared range into a game of RaceFever. Meanwhile, at the head of the conference table, their boss continued to rattle on about the company's web site, oblivious to the silent wireless chatter all around him.

The CEO of a client urgently requested that a senior manager contact a bankrupt competitor and offer assistance in servicing its pending jobs. Ignoring his request cost the company as much as $500,000 in lost revenue.

Level One, Pretending, is appearing to listen when you really don't. It is ignoring with the added dimension of hypocrisy. People who pretend to listen at least recognize that they *should* be listening—that's why they pretend. Usually we pretend to listen when a speaker is going on too long, when we have to listen to someone in authority, or when we listen to someone on the phone while we surf the Web, check our e-mail, or do other "multi-tasking." (Do yourself a big favor: don't do multi-tasking whenever your spouse calls. If you don't believe me, try it. You'll see.)

"There's not a meeting I go to where I'm not reading my e-mail or playing a game," says Gibson, the Handango marketing exec. "It's the only way to stay awake sometimes." Another high-tech marketing executive who shall remain anonymous plays

Tetris on his Newton during meetings. "The best thing is that no one thinks you are goofing off—it looks like you are taking lots of notes," he says. "You do have to master the art of the well-timed nod, though." This secret goofing off at meetings is so rampant that *Fortune* magazine published five "Signs Your Workers Are Toying Around":

1. Guilty looks (the kind any parent would recognize)
2. Inappropriate laughter in meetings
3. Jumpiness—they are easily startled
4. Gadget fumbling whenever a supervisor passes by
5. Trancelike states.[31]

This is all pretty funny, but pretending can take place on a larger and more devious scale. A few years ago, a large pharmaceutical corporation conducted an internal compulsory survey designed to "listen to our employees," but the survey results were subjected to such a spin that many employees felt duped. For example, the company boasted that 46 percent of its employees responded that they believed management to be willing to give up short-term gain in order to do the right thing. This means that the other 54 percent, over half of the company's employees, believed the exact opposite: that management is more committed to quick gains than doing the right thing—a fact the company pretended to ignore. One middle manager quietly called the survey "a complete farce" and left the company shortly thereafter. Management would have done well to stop pretending and to pay attention to the serious indictment over half its workforce was communicating. But management chose pretending over listening.

Will was trying to entice any Palm-wielding colleague into a game of RaceFever. Meanwhile, their boss continued to rattle on about the company's website, oblivious to the silent wireless chatter all around him.

Level Two: Controlling

Controlling is listening that influences—through gestures, facial expressions, or sounds—what the speaker can say. Authority figures such as senior executives, judges, professors or doctors often have a Level Two effect, whether wittingly or unwittingly. They suppress what people can get out of their mouth. Have you ever had the experience of trying to speak to the boss and feeling slightly inadequate? Even if you did not stutter and stumble, did you feel like you couldn't find the right words, and ultimately you said what your listener wanted to hear, not quite what was 100 percent true for you? That is what it feels like to be listened to in a controlling way.

The mere presence of an authority figure can be controlling, even if that person has no intention of controlling what others say.

The mere presence of an authority figure can be controlling, even if that person has no intention of controlling what others say. The chairman of the board of one of our clients once attended the weekly Business Development teleconference. Even though he had no intention of controlling what the participants said—he was genuinely there to learn more about the company's products so that he could represent them to second-round financiers—his presence on the call turned out to be controlling. Account executives were afraid of saying something that would make them look incompetent. Before anyone could say "good morning," the call had lost its usual momentum and fun.

Or take Michael Cowpland, the boss of the software maker Corel, who admits that his kinetic energy and top-down management style used to leave his subordinates feeling that their own opinions hardly mattered. "For example, we have an executive meeting every Thursday, and as far as I'm concerned, it's always been a level playing field—99 percent consensus—but the thing is, other people see it differently," Cowpland recalled. "If I was saying one thing, they might be too intimidated to put forward another strong opinion." What was his solution? "To create a platform for other people—whether we institute votes or minutes, or get someone else to run the agenda—so that each individual or group within the company feels it's being represented."[32]

Tip. Listen for subtle signs that your presence may constrain others in their self-expression.

Level Three: Projecting

Projecting means responding to your own interpretation of what is said, rather than to what the speaker is actually saying. This level is still a counter-productive listening mode. When you project, it is as if you put on your own private light show in the movie-theater of your mind. Your projector is running, and it projects your own movie onto the screen instead of seeing it as what

When you project, it is as if you put on your own private light show in the movie-theater of your mind.

it is—a blank screen. We do that every day. When you project, you hear a communication through the filter of your own prior judgments or decisions. You hear what you want to hear. You project that the speaker is suspicious or innocent, stupid or clever, ugly or gorgeous, difficult or malleable. Whatever the speaker says reinforces and builds evidence for your prior judgments.

An episode of the television show *Seinfeld* is a good example of projecting in particular and the power of listening in general. A woman friend is convinced that George Costanza is crazy and needs psychiatric help. No matter what George says or does, it is only further evidence to her that he is insane. Of course, he is committed to a mental hospital by mistake, and the woman shows up. Relieved, George pleads with her desperately: "Get me out of here. You, of all people, would know that I'm not crazy." The woman just smiles at him sadly, and we see in that instance that she now has the ultimate evidence of George's insanity. This woman can see nothing but signs that he is insane. She has no clue that she—and more precisely her interpretation—has anything to do with what she is seeing and hearing. To her, George's craziness is real.

Several directors at a client became convinced that the new CEO was unable to lead the firm. Everything he did or said became further evidence that he was incapable.

The effects of projection and selective listening are just as dramatic, and much less entertaining, in real life. Several directors at a client became convinced that the new CEO was unable to lead the firm. Everything he did or said became further evidence that he was incapable. They never said this to his face; they just listened to whatever he said or did with that interpretation. Their projecting put him on the defensive; he had no chance to lead without fear or doubt.

But it takes two to tango. The CEO was not a victim. He was guilty of projecting too. He started to second-guess himself. He tended to hear anything around him—that the Board hired a new general manager, that employees in another city informed him of a strategy session at the last minute—as evidence of a conspiracy against him. "They think I am a failure, and they are trying to force me out." Projecting had become a vicious cycle with a "reality" from which escape was next to impossible. I finally had to confront the directors and ask them to say their concerns directly to the CEO so he could do something about them instead of being the victim of their projection.

Tip. Consider which "realities" in your life might be your own projections. Which people and situations show up the way they do simply because of your own interpretations? Catch yourself whenever you think or say, "This person / situation is..." Instead, practice thinking or saying, "In my interpretation, this person/situation shows up as..."

Level Four: Respecting

Ignoring, Pretending, Controlling, and Projecting were all below-the-line levels of poor and damaging listening. We had to go deep into destructive listening modes. Now we finally get to base camp, and the Matterhorn's majestic peak is in sight for the first time. Respecting is the first level of listening that deserves to be called productive. It is simply hearing the content of a communication—nothing more, nothing less—and responding to what is actually said.

> How many times did you ask someone a question, and all you needed was a "yes" or "no" answer—but instead you got a long explanation you had not asked for?

But that sounds easier than it is. How many times did you ask someone a question, and all you needed was a "yes" or "no" answer—but instead you got a long explanation you had not asked for? You wanted to know "A" and the person gave you "A to K but also Q and B." You ask, "can you get this product to market within three months?" All they have to say is "yes" or "no" or "I don't know." What they say instead is, "we need a different strategy, we are under-resourced, I am losing talent left and right." Pardon the metaphor, but I want to insult this rampant behavior: they say whatever burps up within them. It all is vaguely connected to your question, but you have to dig through a lot of mud to get to the gold. All too often, people do not hear what someone says and instead cloud the communication with their own agenda.

Perhaps we can learn something from history here. The leaders of the ancient Greek city-states sent their envoys to negotiations in foreign lands. Since there were no recording devices or written contracts, their job was to listen carefully to what was said and, once they returned, to present to their leaders what they had heard word for word, nothing more, nothing less. Envoys were not permitted to interpret—only to hear and transmit communications precisely. In a manner of speaking, they were human tape recorders, trained to listen and to re-create. An error of interpretation could cost an envoy his life. Perhaps we would pay attention more closely to what others say if we were killed for failing to listen.

People in our communication trainings are not killed, but this playback exercise is useful. We pair people up and have speaker A say a sentence to listener B, with the simple instruction for B to repeat precisely what A just said. You wouldn't believe what comes out of people's mouths. The results are often hilarious when people cannot remember for the life of them what they just heard, and instead make things up.

Observe what you are doing. Are you waiting for the speaker to finish? Are you thinking of what you will say next instead of focusing on what the speaker is saying? Is your mind wandering?

How do you make the move from projecting your own interpretations onto what you hear to listening respectfully? The answer is twofold: by observation and by constant approximation. David S. Pottruck, the president and co-chief executive of Charles Schwab, the financial services company, admits: "Unless I watch it, I can be overwhelming." He writes that he has concentrated, with evident success, on "listening to hear rather than to answer."[33] Do it like Pottruck and observe what you are doing. Are you waiting for the speaker to finish? Are you thinking of what you will say next instead of focusing on what the speaker is saying? Are you judging the speaker's words, listening for what's wrong? Is your mind wandering? In every conversation, exercise the muscle of real one-to-one listening. Stop thinking about whatever you said earlier or whatever you will say next, and grant the speaker your full, undivided attention now.

> **Tip.** As you listen in conversations, re-create the words you hear silently in your head. In a business meeting, a great way of paying attention is to take notes of what you hear. Remember: you don't lose power if you respect others and their words—quite the contrary. If it works for powerhouses like Jack Welch and Larry Bossidy, it may work for you, too.

Level Five: Empathizing

Believe it or not, even the US Postal Service is beginning to listen. Lack of communication at the vast government agency used to frustrate employees so much that a few of them actually went berserk, adding the term "going postal" to the American vocabulary on violence. And violence was only the tip of the iceberg. By 1997, internal complaints had reached the incredible level of 30,000 a year. Executives realized they needed to do something. The agency's mediation program, aptly named "Redress," produced an unprecedented breakthrough: from September 1998 through June 2000, 17,645 informal disputes were mediated; 80 percent of them were resolved. During the same time, formal complaints, which had peaked in 1997 at 14,000, dropped by 30 percent. The lawyers who started Redress out of a class-action lawsuit in 1994 estimated that the program had saved the agency millions of dollars in legal costs and improved productivity, to say nothing of gains in job satisfaction. "We have found that companies are very interested in transformative mediation," said one of the lawyers, Cynthia Hallberlin, "because of its promise to not just solve the problem at hand, but to help the parties communicate more effectively in the future."

> Lack of communication at the US Postal Service used to frustrate employees so much that a few of them actually went berserk, adding the term "going postal" to the American vocabulary on violence.

How did the Postal Service do this? Redress's success had a lot to do with empathizing. Often, employees simply wanted understanding, or for a boss to apologize. One mediation case involved a postal supervisor and an employee, both women, one white and one black, neither willing to back down. The dispute was over the employee's repeated lateness, but the real issue was about a lack of communication. After yelling at each other for one and a half hours, the two became quiet. Elaine Kirsch, the outside mediator, took the opportunity to point out that the two had more in common than they had thought. Once the supervisor and employee returned to hammering out particular issues, suddenly one of them said words to this effect: "You never lied. You always say what you mean." The ice was broken. It turned out that the employee was often late because she had trouble finding care for her asthmatic child. She

Empathizing requires seeing things from the speaker's point of view.

agreed to call her supervisor when this happened, and the supervisor agreed to be more understanding.[34]

Empathizing requires seeing things from the speaker's point of view. What does the speaker want? What is the point she wants to make? What is the issue he is trying to resolve? You have got to stand in the speaker's shoes.

John F. Kennedy's famous 1963 speech in Berlin is one of the best-known examples of a leader using empathy. The young president created an instant bond with the citizens of the embattled and divided city by saying to 150,000 cheering Berliners:

Two thousand years ago the proudest boast was *Civis Romanus sum.* Today, in the world of freedom, the proudest boast is *Ich bin ein Berliner....* All free men, wherever they may live, are citizens of Berlin, and, therefore, as a free man, I take pride in the words, *Ich bin ein Berliner.*

Back in the United States, another great leader knew how to empathize. Kennedy's contemporary and negotiating opponent Martin Luther King, with his uncanny ability to stand in Kennedy's shoes, knew what the President really needed: to convince the nonaligned nations to join the West and rebuff socialism. At St. John's Church in Birmingham, Alabama, King said in May 1963:

The United States is concerned about its image. When things started happening down here, Mr. Kennedy got disturbed. For Mr. Kennedy... is battling for the minds and the

45

hearts of men in Asia and Africa—some one billion men in the neutralist sector of the world—and they aren't gonna respect the United States of America if she deprives men and women of the basic rights of life because of the color of their skin. Mr. Kennedy *knows* that.[35]

Precisely because he empathized with Kennedy, King knew how to exploit his knowledge of the president's situation for his own cause. But he did not use his empathy merely for scheming: he stood in a much more profound place. Once he remarked: "Returning hate for hate multiplies hate, adding deeper darkness to a night already devoid of stars. Darkness cannot drive out darkness; only light can do that. Hate cannot drive out hate, only love can do that."

At level 5, Empathizing, you don't merely listen to a communication's apparent content. Empathizing means that you hear also the intention driving a communication from underneath. Mother Pollard, who was like a mother to the 1960s civil rights leaders, showed her empathy for a weary Martin Luther King, Jr. when she said to him in the middle of a church mass rally:

"Come here, son." King walked over to her and Pollard embraced him with a motherly hug. "Something is wrong with you," she said. "You didn't talk strong tonight."

"Oh no, Mother Pollard," said King, trying to keep up appearances. "Nothing is wrong. I am feeling as fine as ever."

"Now you can't fool me," she said. "I knows something is wrong. Is it that we ain't doing things to please you? Or is it that the white folks is bothering you?"

Before King could say anything, Pollard moved close to his face and said loudly, "I done told you that we is with you all the way. But even if we ain't with you, God's gonna take care of you." With that, she went slowly back to her seat, the crowd roared, and King's eyes filled with tears. He said later that her words, which re-created completely his best sermons, had inspired in him fearlessness in the form of raw energy.[36]

Empathizing is useful in domains other than politics. Take sports: Joe Torre, the seasoned manager of the New York Yankees who led the team to four World Series titles, is known not for clubhouse blowups or emotional outbursts, but for his people skills. He says: "I don't react to what players say. They often say things out of frustration. I want to know why they say it."[37]

Claiborne went beyond the level of respecting to empathizing: listening for the consumer's intentions was one of her biggest weapons in beating her competition.

Needless to say, empathizing is essential to business. You can only succeed if you stand in the shoes of your customers, competitors and suppliers. The clothing designer Liz Claiborne became one of the most successful fashion entrepreneurs in part because of her ability to

empathize with her customers. Claiborne listened carefully to—or, more precisely, *for*—what her customers wanted. "I listened to the customer. I went on the selling floor as a saleswoman, went into the fitting room, heard what they liked and didn't like. Not that you do exactly what they want. What you do is digest the information and then give them what you think they ought to have." This is where Claiborne went beyond the level of respecting to empathizing: she didn't listen one-to-one, she listened for the consumer's *intentions*. Her sensitivity to the needs and desires of her customers was one of her biggest weapons in beating her competition. Once, when Claiborne did not listen carefully and put out miniskirts, she paid the price: "We discovered that our customer is a bit older and a bit more conservative than we thought."[38] Her customers went elsewhere.

The problem is that empathizing is a creative act, and it is difficult to make into a routine. Standard operating procedures, for example, are hardly suited for empathy. Dawn Barbour, a customer service representative for Verizon, then Bell Atlantic, learned this the hard way. She had delivered outstanding customer service: she had just made an angry customer stop ranting, solved his problem, and even elicited a kind word. "I hate Bell Atlantic, but you're the nicest rep I ever had," the caller said. Barbour would have liked to simply say "Thank you." But she had to follow a script. "Did I provide you with outstanding service today?" she inquired. That's when the customer lost it all over again. "Isn't that what I just said?" he barked. "I felt like a total idiot," Barbour said later. But customer service agents were required to ask the "outstanding service" question at the end of every call, she said, and if she had dropped it, a supervisor listening in could have deducted points from her performance score, reducing her chance of a promotion[39] (Verizon has since changed that rigid procedure). The lesson is that you cannot legislate or regulate empathy: it's where you come from, not what you say.

> **Empathizing enables you to respond by facilitating the other person's intention. If you hear not only what the person is saying, but also the intention behind the words, you bring power to your response and serve the speaker and yourself.**

Empathizing enables you to respond by facilitating the other person's intention. If you hear not only what the person is saying (or yelling, as the case may be), but also the intention behind the words, you bring power to your response and serve the speaker and yourself.

Note that I have said "response," not "reaction." The difference between the two is significant. When you react, you are like a dog that barks whenever the other dog barks. Janette Mandell, who coaches executives on their media appearances, once led a mock session in which she told a software CEO that her "sources" had leaked that he was planning to sell the company. "His eyes grew wide and he leapt out of his seat and barked, 'Who told you that!'" she said. "When the whole room erupted in laughter, he knew he had made a big mistake.[40] You are in the grip of your emotions, and you reciprocate at the same level—an eye for an eye. If you feel you have been insulted, you insult the person back. By contrast, when you respond, you can step back, try to reveal the intention behind the communication, and act accordingly. In response to a seeming insult, you might ask, "I can hear you're frustrated. What's upsetting you?" or "I can understand how you would feel this way. What can I do to help?" When you stand in the other person's shoes and try seeing the world through her eyes, you can see why she behaves as she does. Reacting only escalates conflict. By responding empathetically, you can resolve conflicts more quickly and permanently.

There are times when you must speak up, for example to prevent injustice. The point is to do so deliberately and by choice, and not in an automatic or emotional reaction.

When you clash with another person, try to step back and look at the interaction in a larger context. Try saying to yourself, "This person and I might work together for decades to come. What can I do right now to build a deeper partnership for the future?" Viewing things from a larger perspective frees you from being the victim of your knee-jerk reactions. You have lifted the conversation to a higher level. This is not to suggest that you should never raise your voice. There are times when you must speak up, for example to prevent injustice. The point is to do so deliberately and by choice, and not in an automatic or emotional reaction.

> **Tip.** Whatever they are saying to you, remember: they are probably not responding to you. You don't have to play their game. When things turn sour, attempt to elevate the conversation to a higher plane.

Level Six: Generating

Now we come to a highly sophisticated level of listening. Generating is active, inventive listening that evokes the best qualities in others. When you listen generatively, you create another's brilliance.

Early in her career, Mary Kay Ash, who later became the founder of Mary Kay Cosmetics and one of the most successful women entrepreneurs of the twentieth century, experienced all the levels of listening on herself, all the way from being handicapped to being empowered. As a young saleswoman, Ash was hampered by the lack of respect she received from male colleagues who treated her as a secretary, dismissed her ideas or simply ignored her. But when she went to her first sales conference, she was astounded by the awards and recognition bestowed on successful salespeople. She yearned to be "the Queen of Sales," the title given to the top saleswoman of the previous year. Emboldened by the conference, she marched up to the president, Frank Stanley Beveridge, and told him she was going to become his best sales rep: "Next year I am going to be the Queen." His response took her by surprise: "He took my hand and held it for a moment, looked me squarely in the eye, and said: 'You know, somehow I think you will.'" According to Ash, Beveridge's words changed her life.[41] I think that, even more important than what he said, what changed everything was how he listened to her commitment. Perhaps for the first time in her life, Ash had the experience of being heard as who she was—and who she could be.

> **Tip.** What if you could design how people show up in your life? Write down the names of a few people you know—colleagues, friends, loved ones, leaders, even people who have died. Next, identify how you currently listen to each one. How does the person show up for you currently? Then, in a second step, design your future listening of each person on your list. How could you listen to each one from now on?

Level Seven: Mastery—Listening to Their Listening

We can now make the final ascent to the peak of the "Matterhorn of Masterful Listening." *You can shape how others listen to you.* Being aware of how others listen to you means being a masterful communicator. Great leaders often distinguish themselves by their ability to hear how their speaking is received *while they speak.* They constantly tailor what they say to their audience. At a more profound level, they are

Great leaders often distinguish themselves by their ability to hear how their speaking is received while they speak.

able to let the audience *speak through them.* They give voice to their listeners' unspoken thoughts and desires, and become a membrane through which their audience gains a voice. That is part of what great leadership is about—giving voice to people who have none. Perhaps that is what Confucius meant when he said that a great leader follows.

Adapting your words to your audience does not mean you are selling out. You adjust your style, never the essence or intention of your speaking. Martin Luther King learned early on to read audiences of every composition. In a speech to an enormous assembly of overwhelmingly white AFL-CIO delegates at the union's annual conference, King stood in their shoes while standing his ground. The union delegates were at best indifferent, and at worst hostile, to his cause when King began. "Negroes are almost entirely a working people," King said, instantly creating common ground between his movement and his listeners, who were all workers too. "There are pitifully few Negro millionaires and few Negro employers." In just two sentences, King had made the struggle for civil rights a part of the class struggle. Having created a bond between the working class and African-Americans, he made his pitch: he asked that union members rigorously root out racial discrimination in their midst. "I am aware that this is not easy nor popular," King conceded, "but the eight-hour day was not popular or easy to achieve." Neither, he pointed out, were child labor acts or the minimum wage. "Out of such struggle for democratic rights you won both economic gains and the respect of the country," he said, "and you will win both again if you make

In your own leadership, train yourself to listen to how others listen to you.

Negro rights a great crusade."[42] King was able to turn his listeners into friends by stepping into their shoes and giving voice to their own unspoken pride in the hard-fought reforms they had won. The AFL-CIO was to become a key ally in the struggle for civil rights.

Nike Inc. committed a major faux-pas—the opposite of listening to others' listening—when it placed several ads for Nike ACG Air Dri-Goat in several national and nine regional outdoor magazines. The ads referred to people with disabilities as "drooling and misshapen." Naturally, disabilities-rights groups were not pleased. "The ad expressed the kind of antiquated bias we are fighting to eradicate," said Mark Kleid, channel producer at a Web site for people with disabilities. Nike was forced to pull the ad. The company could have saved millions of dollars in sunk costs, not to speak of reputation costs, had it listened to what its audience might be thinking.[43]

In your own leadership, train yourself to listen to how others listen to you. Develop the skill of hearing the subtle signals and signs that show you the way and show you what to say. In short, try to address the listening present in the room or on the call. You obviously cannot do this by sticking only to prepared remarks. If you can sidestep your written agenda, your words will come from what your listeners need and want, and your speaking will be in tune with what needs to be said at any given time to produce the outcomes you and they need. Remember that even King, in his history-making "I Have a Dream" speech, had to stray from his prepared speech and allow himself to dance with his listeners. Only then did his dream create a furor in America.

Of course your pre-existing agenda is necessary, but not enough for masterful communication. Your listening *while speaking* has to be the compass that determines how you navigate your remarks. To do this, you need to find a way to stand in your audience's shoes. Rather than focusing on what you have to say, concentrate on what your listeners are hearing, how they see the world, what they are thinking. Then speak to that. Even if you make mistakes, you will probably create more excitement, not to mention a deep rapport with your listeners because they will sense that you are there for them. It's like playing at a jam session—you are not merely replaying music that has worked in the past. Your listeners are present at the creation.

Tip. Imagine how people you speak with are listening to you. Step into their shoes and listen with their ears. Let go of what you are about to say, and listen to their listening.

But what do you do if the opposite happens, and people are not listening when you speak? What do you do when you yourself are the boss who is talking on and on about the company web site while your subordinates are secretly playing with their Blackberries and Palms and pagers? How do you respond if people start to nod off while you are addressing a group, or if you discover in a videoconference that some participants have put the mute button on to talk among themselves? Several responses are possible. You can say, "I know this is a lot of information. Thank you for making it work and staying with me." You can call a break, ask the audience to stand up and stretch for a minute, ask for questions or ask a provocative question yourself—in the videoconference, you may want to ask the very people that have gone "out to lunch." If you empathize with your audience, you will know

Climbing the Matterhorn is hard work and requires a lot of sustained practice for quite some time. Be patient with yourself and others.

what is missing and what to say. Remember that your speaking can give voice to the audience's unexpressed thoughts. You make them feel that they are expressing themselves. You could go around the room or videoconference and let everyone speak, but that could take hours. You can accomplish the same thing in seconds by speaking to the listening that you hear as you speak.

Don't worry if this business of hearing while speaking doesn't work out right away. I did not choose the metaphor of climbing the Matterhorn by accident. Climbing the Matterhorn is hard work and requires *a lot* of sustained practice for quite some time. Be patient with yourself and others.

Also, remember that when you and your team climb a mountain, your expedition is as weak as your weakest link. Leading by example is the place to start, and you should definitely incorporate the levels of listening into your own work before you try to shape up other people's listening. But that is not enough. If possible, make sure that your team members get the chance to train themselves in these distinctions. Ultimately, to cause a breakthrough in team performance, the whole team must climb the Matterhorn, not you alone.

Tip. Experiment for at least a week with the question: What outcomes can I generate through my listening alone?

Lab.

Write down the names of people you know or know of. These can be people with whom you work, friends, loved ones, heads of state, even people who have died. Next, identify how you currently listen to each person. How does each person show up for you? Then, identify how you could listen to each. Actively create your listening of each person on your list.

Person	Current Listening	Possible Future Listening
Bobby White	"When is he gonna finish talking?"	"Where is the gold?"

Now turn the tables: imagine how the people you listed listen to you. Step into their shoes and listen with their ears.

Person	Current Listening	Possible Future Listening

Intermezzo: Yes, You *Can* Listen Too Much

In one communication workshop, an executive asked me: "Why should I listen to my people? What if they come up with baloney?" The executive had a point. Listening is not always right. There are times when you had better interrupt someone who is hijacking the situation, who harbors a malicious intention, or who is speaking a dangerous idea into existence. There are times when too much

In one communication workshop, an executive told me: "Why should I listen to my people? What if they come up with baloney?" The executive had a point.

listening leads to indecision and management by committee, not leadership. Sometimes even listening to your customers today can be detrimental to your company's future, because your customers may not know what they're missing. A breakthrough innovation like Post-Its would probably not have happened by asking customers, because they did not know they wanted yellow stickies. On the whole, however, we tend to err in the opposite direction: we don't listen enough. Far more damage is done by not listening enough than by listening too much. The following story, sent to me by a friend, is a delightful illustration of the emotional knots we all tie ourselves when we don't listen rigorously. Enjoy this little cookie break before we go into the next section, **Speaking for Results**.

> Let's say Ned is attracted to a woman named Jennifer. He asks her out to a movie; she accepts; they have a pretty good time. A few nights later he asks her out to dinner, and again they enjoy themselves. They continue to see each other regularly, and after a while neither one of them is seeing anyone else.

> And then, one evening when they are driving home, a thought occurs to Jennifer; without really thinking, she says it aloud: "Do you realize that, as of tonight, we've been seeing each other for exactly six months?" And then there is silence in the car. To Jennifer, it seems like a very loud silence.

> She thinks to herself: Geez, I wonder if it bothers him that I said that. Maybe he's feeling confined by our relationship; maybe he thinks I'm trying to push him into some kind of obligation that he doesn't want, or isn't sure of.

> And Ned is thinking: Gosh, six months.

And Jennifer is thinking: But, hey, I'm not sure I want this kind of relationship, either. Sometimes, I wish I had a little more space, so I'd have time to think about whether I really want us to keep on going the way we are, moving steadily forward...I mean, where are we going? Are we just going to keep seeing each other at this level of intimacy? Are we heading for marriage? Toward children? Toward a lifetime together? Am I ready for that level of commitment? Do I really know this person?

And Ned is thinking:...so that means it was...let's see...February when we started going out, which was right after I had the car at the dealer's, which means,...Let me check the odometer...whoa! I am way overdue for an oil change here.

And Jennifer is thinking: He's upset. I can see it on his face. Maybe I am reading this completely wrong. Maybe he wants more from our relationship, more intimacy, more commitment; maybe he has sensed—even before I sensed it—that I was feeling some reservations. Yes, I bet that's it. That's why he's so reluctant to say anything about his own feelings. He's afraid of being rejected.

And Ned is thinking: And I'm gonna have them look at that transmission again, too. I don't care what those morons say, it's still not shifting right. And they better not try to blame it on the cold weather this time. What cold weather? It's 87 degrees out, and this thing is shifting like a garbage truck, and I paid those incompetent thieves $600.

And Jennifer is thinking: He's angry. And I don't blame him. I'd be angry too. God, I feel so guilty putting him through this, but I can't help the way I feel. I'm just not sure.

And Ned is thinking: They'll probably say it's only a 90-day warranty. That's exactly what they will say, the scum-balls.

And Jennifer is thinking: Maybe I'm just too idealistic, waiting for a knight to come riding up on a white horse, when I'm sitting right next to a perfectly decent person, a person who I enjoy being with, a person who I care about, a person who truly cares about me. A person who is in pain because of my self-centered, schoolgirl romantic fantasy.

And Ned is thinking: Warranty? They want a warranty? I'll give them a warranty. I'll take their warranty and stick it right up their...

"Ned," Jennifer says aloud.

"What?" says Ned, startled.

"Please don't torture yourself like this," she says, her eyes beginning to brim with tears.

"Maybe I should never...oh God, I feel so..." She breaks down, sobbing.

"What?" says Ned.

"I'm such a fool." Jennifer sobs. "I mean, I know there's no knight. I really know that. It's silly. There's no knight, and there's no horse."

"There's no horse?" says Ned.

"You think I'm a fool, don't you?" Jennifer says.

"No!" says Ned, glad to finally know the correct answer.

"It's just...it's that I...I need some time," Jennifer says.

There is a fifteen-second pause while Ned, thinking as fast as he can, tries to come up with a safe response. Finally, he comes up with what he thinks might work.

"Yes," he says.

A befuddled pause.

"Oh Ned, do you really feel that way?" she says.

"What way?" says Ned.

"That way about time," says Jennifer.

"Oh," says Ned. "Yes."

Jennifer turns to face him and gazes deeply into his eyes, causing him to become very nervous about what she might say next, especially if it involves a horse. At last, she speaks.

"Thank you, Ned," she says.

We think we are good at speaking because we all speak every day and have done it all our lives.

"Thank you," says Ned, more confused than ever.

Then he takes her home, and she lies on her bed, a conflicted, tortured soul, and weeps until dawn. Whereas, when Ned gets back to his place, he opens a bag of Doritos, turns on the TV, and immediately becomes deeply involved in a rerun of a tennis match between two Czechoslovakians he has never even heard of. A tiny voice in the far recesses of his mind tells him something major was going on back there in the car, but he is pretty sure he would never understand, and he figures it's better if he doesn't think about it.

The next day, Jennifer will call one of her closest friends, or perhaps two of them, and they will talk about this situation for weeks. For six straight hours, in painstaking detail, they will analyze everything she said and everything he said, going over it time and time again, exploring every word, expression, and gesture for nuances of meaning, considering every ramification. They will continue to discuss this subject, off and on, for weeks, maybe months, never reaching definite conclusions, but never getting bored with it either.

Meanwhile, Ned, while working on his car with a mutual friend of his and Jennifer's, will pause, frown, and say, "Did Jennifer ever own a horse?"

To prevent such miscommunications from damaging your enterprise, and as a little workout for your listening muscles, experiment with the listening tips in Table 2.

Listening Tips.

- Focus on what is being said without thinking about what you are going to say next.

- Listen without a point of view. Avoid immediate free-association to your own experience. Put your tendency to evaluate on hold.

- Listen and mentally re-create exactly what the speaker is saying.

- See things from the other person's point of view.

- Listen for the speaker's underlying intention.

- Listen for "gold": hear whatever the person is saying as the solution to the issue being discussed.

- Listen one minute longer than may be comfortable.

- Experiment with listening. What results can you produce through listening rather than talking?

- Remember that your advice is usually noise to their ears. People are not eager for your speaking. They are hungry for your listening.

Table 2: Listening Tips.

Now that we have some understanding of the listening aspect of communication, we can deal with the other side of the coin. We think we are good at speaking because we all speak every day and have done it all our lives. But if I may be so bold: in truth, for most of us, our speaking ability is sub-par. Let me show you what I mean.

Chapter 4

Speaking for Results

Words have come to be very cheap, particularly in our circles.
They ceased to be commitments.
Gone is the sensitivity to their power.

Abraham J. Heschel

The meeting did not go well, to say the least.

It started when Bill Gates said to AOL's Steve Case, "I can buy 20 percent of you or I can buy all of you. Or I can go into this business myself and bury you."

The informal meeting in May 1993 was meant to explore a possible collaboration between the two companies; but to AOL executives, Gates' words sounded more like an outright threat. The words "bury you" rang in their ears—and they immediately went on the defensive. Case fired back, "The company's not for sale." Gates was surprised, according to Russell Siegelman, the executive in charge of building Microsoft's online capacity who had set up the meeting. As he saw it, Gates was simply laying out the range of options Microsoft had to consider as it ventured into the online arena. "Gates wasn't obnoxious or combative," said Siegelman. "He didn't mean, 'I'm gonna crush you.' He meant that he was interested in this area and wanted to find the right way to leverage the technology for Microsoft and figure out the best direction to go in." If that was Gates' intention, he did a terrible job at communicating it. He was honest, yes; but

It started when Bill Gates said to AOL's Steve Case, "I can buy 20 percent of you or I can buy all of you. Or I can go into this business myself and bury you."

whether he meant to or not, his words created a mood of adversity and danger, and people went up in arms.

Gates, one of the greatest entrepreneurs of the twentieth century (and likely of the twenty-first), had long been hampered by poor communication skills. The director of Harvard's computer lab said that Gates had been "a hell of a good pro-

People say stupid things when their livelihood is up for grabs.

grammer" as a student, but "an obnoxious human being... He'd put people down when it was not necessary, and just generally not be a pleasant fellow to have around the place."[44] Although he learned a lot of social skills as Microsoft grew, Gates was still not exactly a calibrated communicator. One journalist who spent several months as a fly-on-the-wall at the company wrote about how the chairman "exploded in anger," leaving a "palpable nervousness in the room."[45]

Now Gates was doing it again—and his words fell on fertile ground for misinterpretation. It takes two to mess up communication, and Steve Case and the other AOL executives certainly did their part. They were apprehensive and expected signs of warfare. "We didn't trust Microsoft's motives, because we knew they could emerge as a major competitor," Case said later. "At one point in the meeting, Siegelman proposed a 50-50 joint venture, but from our point of view, it was 'OK, we'll help build it, teach you all about it, then just when it gets interesting, you'll shoot us.'"[46]

This is a perfect example of how wars break out—software wars and wars with guns and bullets. Similar exchanges take place in thousands of meetings every week; and with economic uncertainty on the rise, expect more of these exchanges. People say stupid things when their livelihood is up for grabs. In this case, the meeting launched a war between Microsoft and AOL over absolute dominance in the nascent online services industry. Each side vowed to drive the other out of business. But it didn't have to be this way. What went wrong with the speaking aspect?

Most of us fail to make some basic distinctions in our speaking, and it shows in our communications and ultimately in our results. One simple binary distinction is this: the words we use produce clarity and action—or confusion and powerlessness. That is why I call the distinctions that follow unproductive and productive ways of speaking. Unproductive speaking slows things down, creates confusion and indecision, or disables people and their accomplishments. Unproductive speaking is a source of an unbelievable amount of needless costs and waste. Nobody has quantified the extent of that loss, for example its proportion of GDP, but just from anecdotal evidence we can safely assume that the waste is enormous.

I doubt that any of the terms below will be new to you. But being aware of a term is not the same as being adept at using the distinction. Take "requests." We all know what a request is, but how often do we use requests as a way to create partnership, produce unexpected results, or enable others to go beyond business as usual? More often than not, we assume that we've made a request when all we've done is barked an order or made a vague allusion.

One virtuoso of the vague allusion is my mother. If she is cold and wants the window closed, she will ask my father, "Aren't you cold?" leaving it up to him to figure out what she really wants. And believe me, she is not alone. Look how often managers or board members shy away from making clear requests. Instead they say: "I think..." or "we should have..." or "I can't...," only to set themselves up for later disappointment.

By distinguishing unproductive from productive communications and minimizing the unproductive ones, you become a speaker adept at generating power and purpose. You are then on the path to mastery with language: speaking (or e-mailing, voice mailing or Web casting) in a way that brings about the reality you choose to create. Let's start with the no-no's, the capital sins of speaking.

The Four Deadly Sins of Speaking

The tongue weighs practically nothing.
But so few people can hold it.
Anonymous

The capital sins of unproductive speaking are rumor, judgment, excuse, and threat. These types of speaking have two things in common: they do damage, and they stifle action. The damage is often done unwittingly. When the financial controller at one of our dot-com clients says in frustration, "I can't pay the bills as long as those account executives don't produce sales," her intentions are good. She is even right. But people around her do not experience any opening for action from her threat. All they experience is guilt and blame.

> When the financial controller says, "I can't pay the bills as long as those account executives don't produce sales," her intentions are good. But people around her do not experience any opening for action, only guilt and blame.

Deadly Sin #1: Rumor and Gossip. Rumor and gossip, our first sins of speaking, are usually about the personal affairs of others. A French phrase aptly sums up this way of speaking: *"Les absents ont toujours tort"* ("Those who are gone are always wrong"). The French got it exactly right: rumor and gossip are never communicated directly to the people whom they badmouth. They are at the opposite end of the spectrum from responsibility.

A few careless—or on the contrary, maliciously and carefully placed—words can destroy what took years to build. Rumors and gossip have the power to damage the best organizations. They are possibly the most deadly ways of speaking.[47]

Even if they did no other damage, rumor and gossip are costly at the least. If 1,000 people work for a company, each earns an average of $30 an hour and each spends an hour a day gossiping at the water cooler, over lunch or at the copier, the organization will lose a quarter million a day, or more than $62 million a year. And that figure does not take into account the opportunity costs—opportunities missed while people chatter away.

A few careless— or on the contrary, maliciously and carefully placed— words can destroy what took years to build.

Rumor and gossip rise with bad times, so expect more of them in this next phase of economic uncertainty. The more people sense that their job is on the line, the less straight they will be to your face. Fear will block them from communicating honestly. At one of our clients, people had never been trained to say what they thought to each other's faces. In public, they said only the words they thought their superiors wanted to hear. Two people, the chairman and the CEO, took it to the extreme. Each of them called me overseas—each separately—to talk about the other, when their offices were about a three-minute walk from each other.

As I use the terms, rumor and gossip include complaining about an issue to people who have no power to do something about it. Most of us have that nasty habit. We complain to anyone and everyone except the person who can do something to resolve our complaint. If you are an account executive, complaining to other account executives about the VP of sales will only aggravate your issue, because all you do is gather evidence for your viewpoint instead of speaking to the VP directly. The person who complains only to co-workers who cannot act fuels the perception that "nothing matters," "we have no power to change things," "they never listen," or "life here sucks."

When enough people in an organization add enough of this fuel, the environment begins to mirror their complaints. Of course, the people doing the complaining have no idea that they had everything to do with shaping the environment they so vigorously oppose. They don't see that they literally speak that environment into being.

> Of course, the people doing the complaining have no idea that they had everything to do with shaping the environment they so vigorously oppose.

Speaking irresponsibly is among the most counterproductive things people can do. I call such speaking "ontological pollution," which is at least as damaging as environmental pollution. But rumors not only pollute the environment, they can hamper historic undertakings. Gossip deliberately spread by the FBI and its zealous boss, J. Edgar Hoover—the epitome of a bureaucratic leader with an outsized sense of his mission and a Machiavellian taste for power politics—nearly derailed Martin Luther King's civil rights work. Hoover and his agents were obsessed with the *idée fixe* that Stanley Levison, King's closest white friend and ally, was in reality a Communist agent scheming to subvert the United States. Once the Bureau had spread its innuendo and rumors for long enough, there was no need to prove its allegations. Evidence for the alleged crimes or misdeeds became unnecessary. Simply by contaminating people with stubborn suspicions, the FBI was able to isolate Levison. Finally, he was forced to separate himself from the civil rights movement and his dear friend King, lest he jeopardize their mission. Everyday rumor and gossip may not be as systematic as the FBI's campaign against King, but they can be every bit as undermining.

To support the health and productivity of your enterprise, minimizing rumors and gossip is essential. How can you do that? I recommend three ground rules. First: No gossip. Second: Complain only to the person who can do something about it. That person is usually either the one who gave rise to the issue or the manager in charge. For instance, if you have a complaint about how people are promoted at your company, the person to talk to might be the company president, the department chief or the head of human resources. If that person cannot handle the issue satisfactorily, then you both need to determine a third person who will resolve the issue. The third ground rule: *Offer not a problem, but a solution.* Don't allow people to delegate problems upward in the organization. Hold them accountable for solving problems.

If the climate of secret opinions has become so thick that you can cut the air with a knife, you may need to hold a 360-degree feedback session

If the climate of secret opinions has become so thick that you can cut the air with a knife, you may need to hold a 360-degree feedback session and ask people: "What are you thinking about me [or Joe] that you are not saying?" This solution is certainly a last resort, but it may be necessary to break open an entrenched climate of withheld communications.

> **Tip.** Regardless of your position, refuse to take part in rumor or gossip. Communicate complaints only to people who have the power to resolve them. Offer solutions rather than just stating problems. If others come to you with complaints, ask them to come up with a solution and to talk to someone who can do something about it.

Deadly Sin #2: Judgment and Evaluation. In 1997, David Risher, a fast-rising young Microsoft executive, decided to join an intriguing Internet startup called Amazon.com. Risher's direct superior at Microsoft asked him incredulously: "You're going to leave Microsoft for a retailer?" When Risher was undeterred, he was summoned to Bill Gates' office. He remembers how the Microsoft founder told him quitting was "the stupidest decision you'll ever make." Gates had committed the sin of judgment, and he was dead wrong. Today, Risher is head of all US retail operations and one of Amazon's top ten executives. He is worth around $100 million—after the Amazon stock slump.

Webster gives us several meanings for judgment, including

Judgments need not be negative to do damage.

"the ability to judge, make a decision, or form an opinion objectively, authoritatively, and wisely." In this book, judgment has quite the opposite meaning. It is the act of giving our opinions or conclusions in a way that is subjective, invalid or short-sighted. We judge: "She's too emotional." "He's pushy." "The Web developers just don't get it." "This CEO will never change." "The stupidest decision you'll ever make."

By the way, judgments need not be negative to do damage. You can say, "This new general manager is brilliant," and if that judgment is hyperbolic and inaccurate, it can blind you and others. If a positive judgment keeps you from seeing the facts, it can be every bit as damaging as a negative judgment. Jill Barad's over-confident conclusion as CEO of Mattel that everything was going well for the company, just days before the company was forced to announce a major drop in earnings, ultimately cost her the top job at Mattel.

We all have a tendency to jump to conclusions about others— prominent people like a company leader or a celebrity, and unknowns like another driver in a traffic jam or a new co-worker. We judge people quickly as right or wrong, brilliant or stupid, worthy or unworthy of our attention or our respect. Perhaps television and Hollywood films have taught us that we can size up a person in a few moments. Regardless of why we do it, we box people into a category and ignore their complexities.

We have all judged and been judged. When we judge others, we are righteous, certain, all-knowing. We have no need to understand the whole picture or the circumstances that led to their behavior. We sentence them to the prison of our conclusions. Only when we are judged ourselves can we know how confining that prison can be. Only then do we see how blind

We sentence them to the prison of our conclusions.

righteousness can be and how it feels when people draw conclusions without knowing the facts. Passing judgment on human beings is an effective way to stifle them.

Are you limiting what somebody can do by the very way you characterize them? As an effective leader you must avoid jumping to quick, stereotypical judgments about others. It's not okay to judge people as types. Judging people's actions is better, but still risky. If possible, avoid judgment altogether and instead talk about your experience. "I had the experience of being bypassed by you when you scheduled that meeting without informing me. I know it probably was not your intention, but that was my experience."

Tip. Curb your tendency to judge others. Suspend your inclination to evaluate things or people. Instead, play with this thought: "What if this person were the exact opposite of what I am perceiving them to be? What if they had a perfectly good reason for the behavior that I am judging?

Tip. As you go through your day, think of every statement you say or hear as a commitment. If you catch yourself saying things like "Nobody wants to buy this product" or "I don't trust that guy," ask yourself: am I committed to that interpretation?

Deadly Sin #3: Excuse and Rationalization. An excuse is an explanation or defense that one offers as a reason not to be held accountable. Your business development manager says, "I didn't deliver last month's sales goal because I got the specs from the Web developers too late." "We did our best under the circumstances. What else do you want us to do?" Rationalizing, a close cousin of excuses, implies self-deception and even denial. We rationalize to avoid confronting the truth. "Sure, we knew that software wasn't up to company standards. But what could we do? Management wanted it out by Christmas."

Qui s'excuse, s'accuse ("Those who excuse themselves accuse themselves"— though it sounds way more elegant in French).

Excuses and rationalizations are unproductive for two reasons. First, they are attempts to deflect responsibility by making the speaker look like a victim of overwhelming circumstances. The French language offers an apt description of this aspect of excuses: *Qui s'excuse, s'accuse* ("Those who excuse themselves accuse themselves"—though it sounds way more elegant in French). Second, they over-emphasize the past, generally in an attempt to free us from blame. The problem is, they perpetuate the past—they give us little chance of creating a future that differs from that past.

Tip. Beware of the word "because," whether explicit or implicit. Whatever comes after it is likely an excuse, justification or rationalization.

Deadly Sin #4: Threat and Ultimatum. When your back is against the wall and you see no other method of getting your way, you might resort to the fourth sin of speaking: you threaten an ultimatum. "If this doesn't change, you can always sack me...I'm thinking of leaving anyway." I know a CEO who used to issue this type of ultimatum about every two weeks. Threats are really a sign of weakness, though. They put your listeners on notice that you are on the defensive—not a very smart tactic for a leader. And they create a lot of unnecessary adversity. You separate yourself from everybody else on the team, and you make people see you as an *enfant terrible* that shouldn't be taken seriously.

> **Modes of productive speaking are typically given by a commitment to the future, not the past.**

But enough of the four deadly sins. Before we start beating a dead horse, let's look at something positive: the five secrets of speaking for action and results.

Okay, they are not really secrets. I just call them that because most of us act as if they didn't exist, and we keep getting caught in one of the four deadly sins above. Let's agree on calling them Open Secrets.

Speaking for Results—Six Open Secrets

> *Words do not label things already there.*
> *Words are like the chisel of the carver: they free the idea,*
> *the thing, from the general formlessness of the outside.*
>
> Albert Einstein

Unlike the modes of speaking we just discussed, productive communications empower people and catalyze desired actions and results. They can take the form of declarations or assertions, commitments, requests or invitations, stories—even humor. Unlike unproductive speech, modes of productive speaking commit the speaker to the future, not the past.

I first became familiar with these ways of speaking through the work of The Hunger Project. Our communications had to mobilize a worldwide movement for our mission—ending world

> Whether you work for Banana Republic, Siemens or an Internet boutique, you face huge challenges. You cannot afford to waste time and effort with endless meetings or imprecise speaking.

hunger. Our speaking had to be rigorous. We did not have the luxury of communicating in ways that slowed things down, allowed indecision or undermined people. Our language needed decisiveness and alacrity to empower some 10,000 activists worldwide to take action. Today, the distinctions of speaking we developed are critical to my clients. Whether you work for Banana Republic, Siemens or an Internet boutique, you face huge challenges. You cannot afford to waste time and effort with endless meetings or imprecise or unintentional speaking. If you adopt the Five Open Secrets, your words can bring about the future to which you are committed.

Open Secret #1: Declarations and Assertions. A declaration is generally considered a public, formal announcement. Politicians declare themselves as candidates for public office. This book uses a narrower definition: a declaration is a statement of what will happen in the future, an intention of an unprecedented outcome for which the speaker has no validating evidence. When Colin Marshall declared that British Airways would become the world's premier airline, evidence to validate his declaration was hard to come by. Nothing conveyed the impossibility of Marshall's declaration more than the acronym of British Airways: in the public mind, the initials "BA" stood for "Bloody Awful."

Declarations are useful tools available to leaders. They allow you to express and take steps to manifest vision, commitment, and intention. John F. Kennedy made one of the most famous declarations in modern history when he said in 1961 that the United States would put a man on the moon within a decade and bring him back to Earth safely. Kennedy's declaration spurred the actions that resulted in the first lunar landing in 1969. Even his critics, who deplored the lack of suitable metals for space exploration, the lack of technical know-how, or the lack of money, became a critical part of the effort. Were it not for his declaration, the moon might still be unexplored territory for humanity.

Years before Kennedy became president, he served in World War II, many ranks below General George Marshall. Although by nature a quiet man, Marshall was known for his assertions. He talked straight, even to superiors, which was unheard of in the army (although his

Nothing conveyed the impossibility of Marshall's declaration more than the acronym of British Airways: in the public mind, the initials "BA" stood for "Bloody Awful."

World War I mentor, General Pershing, liked Marshall's frankness). In 1938, when Marshall attended his first briefing at the White House, President Franklin D. Roosevelt presented an ambitious plan for building 10,000 warplanes. Marshall was shocked to realize that Roosevelt had no program for recruiting personnel and servicing the planes. As the president mingled with his guests afterwards, he asked the general whether he had made a good case. Roosevelt was of course fishing for compliments, but he didn't get any from the general. To the consternation of all present, Marshall asserted sharply, "I am sorry, Mr. President, but I don't agree with you at all." His assertion seemed to have ended his career. After the meeting, Treasury Secretary Henry Morgenthau coolly dismissed Marshall, "Well, it's been nice knowing you." It looked as though Marshall's first-ever briefing with the president would be his last. It wasn't. The general, with all his assertions, was to become one of Roosevelt's most trusted advisors. Much of Marshall's credibility derived from two facts. One was that his assertions were invariably well researched. The other was that, as House Speaker Sam Rayburn pointed out, Marshall asserted the truth even when it hurt his own cause.

As I use the term here, an assertion is a statement of commitment for which the speaker can provide evidence. Examples of assertions include a lawyer asserting that her client is innocent, and a corporate executive stating that his firm can develop a new

An assertion is a statement of commitment for which the speaker can provide evidence.

Web-based application by the end of the year. In his article "Managing for Breakthroughs in Productivity," Alan Scherr of IBM calls such fact-based assertions "the fundamental unit of exchange in most large corporate management structures."[48]

Without assertions, declarations are not grounded. After President Kennedy declared that the United States would put a man on the moon, he backed up his declaration with key assertions. He asserted that Congress could allocate the necessary funds, that the know-how was available, and that alloys could be developed to withstand space travel. Kennedy then followed up his words with information and actions. The Apollo program began in 1963, and for the next decade the United States spent $5 billion annually on the space program. The rest is history: on July 20, 1969, Americans Neil Armstrong and Edwin Aldrin landed on the moon, just as Kennedy had declared they would.[49]

Tip: What declaration could you make that would alter the productivity of your team members? "You can pull off this miracle." What assertions should you make to back up your declaration?

Open Secret #2: Commitments and Promises. When Winston Churchill took the helm as Prime Minister in 1940, Britain was on the brink of losing World War II. It looked as though Hitler would dominate Europe, if not the world. But Churchill reversed the course of the war and altered history. The turning point came when he boldly promised on June 4, 1940, in a famous speech to the House of Commons, that the Axis powers would be defeated:

We shall go on to the end, we shall fight in France, we shall fight on the seas and oceans, we shall fight with growing confidence and growing strength in the air, we shall defend our island, whatever the cost may be, we shall fight on the beaches, we shall fight on the landing grounds, we shall fight in the fields and in the streets, we shall fight in the hills; we shall never surrender...[50]

Leaders make outrageous commitments. Bill Gates' lifelong commitment is to solve everyone's computer problems on all the computers worldwide. But whenever I attend management or board meetings, I am amazed at how rarely people use commitments the way Churchill or Gates did. Perhaps they are afraid of sticking their neck out. Whatever the reason, I hear the words "maybe we shouldn't," "I think," "you ought to," or "we can't" much more than the words "I will."

We know that a commitment commits us to do, or not do, something. I use a somewhat more rigorous definition that our clients find invaluable. As we use the term, a commitment is a public declaration to produce a result, and that result needs to meet three criteria: it must be measurable, it must be in time, and it must be unpredictable.

By this definition, commitments must be stated in a way that the outcome can be quantified and verified. In other words, when the promised deadline comes around, it is clear whether you did or did not do what you promised. The more specific a commitment is, the more leverage it has. "I will spend more time with my children" is a vague resolution; "I will read a storybook to my children at least three nights a week" is a commitment. "I promise to make you happy always" is a valid commitment only if the criteria for your happiness are crystal clear to both of us. The words "I promise" or "I commit myself" may be stated ("I commit myself to bringing the streaming software to market by the end of September") or implied ("I'll e-mail the new budget to you this afternoon").

Tip. If you want to produce results beyond the ordinary, make commitments beyond the ordinary—radical commitments that uproot business as usual, commitments that produce butterflies in your stomach when you make them.

A vehicle for extraordinary accomplishment, commitments generate action and enable you to produce more than you would in the absence of making the commitment. Commitments are a potent tool for leaders. Like any other tool, however, commitments are useful only if you know how to use them. You can run into four common pitfalls with commitments:

Pitfall #1 is to use commitments like a magic wand: you make the promise and sit back, waiting for the accomplishment. You can commit to having your portfolio be valued at $10 million by the end of the current quarter; but if you fail to take enough of the right actions to have the result show up, it won't. Promising alone does not ensure accomplishment—far from it. It does enable accomplishment, but only if you follow it up with actions that are a match for the commitment.

Pitfall #2 is to promise too small. Making a commitment creates a gap between the current reality and what we are promising. Most people find that gap unsettling. Failure is always a possibility when you commit yourself to producing a result regardless of the circumstances. To reduce the discomfort, people sometimes try to narrow the gap by lowering their commitment and make it more predictable. The pull to reduce your risk can be enormous. If you are a VP of Business Development who promised $250,000 in sales last month and delivered $194,000, the temptation is great to commit to a safe number next month, say $175,000. But lowering your commitment is not the thing to do. A prediction is predictable while a commitment is visionary. This is not to say that predictions are not useful. Making viable predictions is essential to sound management. Predictions allow for certainty. They are designed for control, for making us feel safe, while commitments allow for producing unprecedented results. Managers make predictions; leaders stick their necks out and promise.

> **Tip.** If you deliver all your commitments, they are not big enough.

Pitfall #3 in promising is to question whether you can really be trusted to do what you said. But promising and trust exist in separate domains. Not fulfilling an unreasonable commitment does not mean that you are untrustworthy or a failure. My trust in you does not depend on whether or not you fulfill your commitments; rather, it depends on you keeping your agreements. When you make big commitments, failure is always a possibility. Commitments enable us, as Theodore Roosevelt put it, to take on the risk of "failing while daring greatly":

> Far better it is to dare mighty things, to win glorious triumphs, even though checkered by failure, than to take rank with those poor spirits who neither enjoy much nor suffer much, because they live in the gray twilight that knows not victory nor defeat.[51]

Pitfall #4, probably the most serious one, is to keep your commitment private. Sometimes you are afraid to look like a fool—or a loser—if you make a public commitment and fail to keep it. So you jot the commitment down for yourself or, worse, make only a mental note of it. Commitments must be made public—or, at the very least, you need to make them to one other person who can hold you to account whenever you feel like giving up. You have got to box yourself in and commit yourself unequivocally to following through on your commitment. That is how your commitments lead you to extraordinary accomplishment. Nokia did this when it promised it would sell 400,000 cell phones by Christmas 1999. Its sales teams got so revved up and took such a flurry of actions that the company ended up selling 20 million. (Okay, maybe the Finns were a bit afraid of making a really bold commitment. Scandinavian commitments are typically over-conservative and come awfully close to mere predictions, as we see in the next chapter.)

Lab

What commitment could you make now that would force you to take a risk, or show a side of yourself that has been hidden from view? What commitment would even reveal an area of current incompetence? To whom could you make that commitment so you are accountable for delivering it?

_____

_____

_____

_____

_____

_____

Open Secret #3: Requests and Invitations. Leaders make not only big commitments, but also big requests—so big as to enable others to go beyond themselves. Ted Turner was famous for giving people at CNN an "impossible task," as his chief financial officer, Will Sanders, recalled. "He was always playing 'You Bet Your Company,'" Sanders, who was often frustrated with Turner's outlandish requests, said. "Every project he took on had the potential to sink him. No sooner did you feel like you were comfortable and able to breathe a little bit than we'd take on some other impossible task."[52]

Requests are the mirror of promises. They are solicitations of commitment, designed to cause others to do something. "I request that you capture at least 20 percent market share for our streaming services this year." Like commitments, true requests are set in time, and the action being requested is quantifiable and verifiable. Requests begin with the words, "I request," although these words are sometimes implied rather than stated, as in "Will you e-mail me the new budget by this afternoon?" or "Please cancel this meeting immediately."

Whatever the reason, many managers miss the opportunity to make powerful requests.

Much like commitments, requests are a vastly under-utilized resource. Einstein said that we utilize only about 10 percent of our brain's capacity; I assert we use only 10 percent of the power available in requests. Although (or because?) requests are a very potent tool of empowerment, we shy away from them. Perhaps we are afraid of that much power. Or maybe we don't want to be intrusive; we'd rather shield people from the fire of their own commitment. Whatever the reason, many managers miss the opportunity to make powerful requests.

Similar to, but weaker than a request, an invitation is defined by Webster as "something offered as a suggestion." To invite means "to ask or request the presence or participation of in a kindly, courteous, or complimentary way." Invitations need not be in time; we sometimes want them to be open-ended. For example, "I invite you to use our customized Web application for your next project."

It is important to distinguish invitations and requests from communications that must be obeyed—orders, commands, or rules. The only acceptable response to such communications is "yes." Drivers don't have options about how they respond to speed-limit signs along highways, just as most office workers don't have a choice about filling out timesheets or starting work at 9 A.M. There are consequences for disobeying rules. If a policy

It is also wise to communicate the background and purpose of the rule so that listeners understand why it exists and don't feel victimized by it, which might let them off the hook.

in your company is that all employees take part in special Business Development campaigns, they do not have the option of accepting or declining to participate. They either take part in the campaigns or find a new job.

With an order, command or rule, the obligation to participate is on the listener, who has no choice but to comply or else....The only obligation of the speaker is to clarify the rule or order and the consequences of noncompliance. It is also wise to communicate the background and purpose of the rule so that listeners understand why it exists and don't feel victimized by it, which might let them off the hook. ("Did you hear the ridiculous demand he made of us today? There's no way I'm gonna deliver this.")

In contrast to an order or rule, when you issue a genuine invitation or request, the listener has a choice to respond by accepting, declining or counter-offering. If you request that an employee participate in a campaign that will entail overtime, she may say "yes," "no," or counter-offer "I will start next week after I complete my current project." This freedom of choice is crucial. Once your colleague answers your request by accepting or counter-offering, their answer becomes their commitment. Unless they experience choice in the matter, their commitment will turn into a sour obligation.

It is the speaker's obligation to communicate the vision behind the request or invitation in such a way that the listener has a real choice to participate. That's why people can go to extraordinary lengths when they make important invitations and requests. They send elegant cards or striking e-mails as invites to parties or product launches. To invite a promising candidate to join your company, you may take her to dinner or lunch. To ask a woman to marry him, a man better get down on his knee. (Luckily, the words "Marry me!" are a request, not a command, in most cultures.)

Tip. Be clear whether you're making a request or issuing an order. If it's an order, your listeners need to comply. If it's a request, they have a choice. No one likes to be strong-armed into accepting a request.

Tip. Be sure to follow up any commitment or request you make. Jack Welch of GE was known for following up on meetings by sending immediate follow-up notes to each participant recapitulating each of their commitments and requests. They knew he knew.

At the risk of repeating myself: leaders make outlandish commitments and requests. The process is simple. First, you state a commitment that is not bound by what you consider feasible or by how things have been done in the past. Steve Case promised that AOL would be the world's leading interactive online company when his company was still behind a garage in the middle of nowhere.

Second, make requests that are commensurate with that commitment. Over and over again, Case challenged his colleagues to produce the unpredictable, whether it was to reach the 10 million-member threshold by 1996 or to keep inventing the most cutting-edge, user-friendly features for AOL members. Nothing leads to extraordinary accomplishment as quickly as outrageous commitments and requests do—as long as you take your words seriously.

Mahatma Gandhi organized his entire life around his commitment to free India from colonial domination. Gandhi had very specific conditions for fulfilling that commitment. One was that the struggle for liberation must be nonviolent, guided by satyagraha

First, state a commitment that is not bound by what you consider feasible or by how things have been done in the past. Second, make requests that are commensurate with that commitment.

(Hindi for "truth grasping") or passive resistance. All his actions were correlated to that commitment, and he made outrageous requests—of the British government as well as of his countrymen.

One request turned out to be the greatest gamble of Gandhi's life—and it very nearly cost him his life itself. In 1948, at the age of 79, he decided to go on a fast: the equivalent of a request of his countrymen to end the civil war raging among them. Gandhi became weaker and weaker day by day. His doctors feared his imminent death as the fighting raged unabated across the subcontinent. Finally, Gandhi's life hung on a thread. His aide Pyarelal Nayar rushed to his residence to deliver the crucial message: the warring parties had signed a peace agreement, and Nayar held in front of Gandhi's face the written pledge to restore "peace, harmony and fraternity between the communities." After giving a sigh of satisfaction, Gandhi asked if all city leaders had signed it. Nayar hesitated, then confessed that two signatures were still missing: those of the two most implacable adversaries, who, the aide assured Gandhi, would sign the next day. Gandhi shook his head. "No," he murmured, "nothing must be done in haste. I will not break my fast until the stoniest heart has melted." Nayar accepted Gandhi's request, the leaders signed that day, the fighting stopped, and Gandhi ended his fast. He had put his life on the line for an outrageous request: the unconditional end of violence in India.

Tip. Whenever you feel sluggish, make outrageous requests of three people. The very act of requesting, of awakening others to their excellence, will wake you up and get you back on the track of leadership.

Open Secret #4: Appreciation and Acknowledgment. One of my favorite axioms in life is this: "What you appreciate gives you power." I call it an axiom because it cannot be proved or disproved, but in my experience it simply works for those who do it. If you adopt this axiom, the biggest obstacle can turn into an opportunity, and the most annoying co-worker can become an ally. What do I mean by this? When you appreciate a person or a situation, or you appreciate why that person or situation is in your life at this moment, you are no longer the victim of your circumstances. By embracing whatever exists, you put yourself into the driver's seat. The poet Rainer Maria Rilke perhaps summed this up best when he wrote a century ago:

> Be patient towards all that is unsolved in your life, and try to love the questions themselves. Do not now seek the answers which cannot be given to you because you would not be able to live them, and the point is to live everything. Live the questions now. Perhaps you will then, gradually, without noticing it, live some long distant day into the answers.

By "acknowledgment," I do not mean "flattery," by the way. Flattery implies wrongful praise. Casanova, for example, taught that you always tell beauty it's intelligent, and intelligence that it's beautiful. Acknowledgment is the opposite of flattery: it recognizes and praises things and people for what they are. Acknowledgment is a magical tool—whatever you acknowledge in a person, you can be sure that they will do more of the precise things for which you acknowledge them. In my experience, those managers who routinely appreciate and acknowledge team members for specific actions or behaviors have reaped rich rewards: their teams regularly go beyond the call of duty and would do almost anything for them. (Women leaders have often been highly skillful in praising men for the very things they want those men to do more of in the future. If you don't know what I mean, ask your women friends.)

> **Tip.** Exercise your muscle of appreciation and acknowledgment. On at least a weekly basis, determine what you can appreciate about your life. Identify whom to acknowledge or thank, and for what.

Open Secret #5: Stories. Leaders often need to inspire, encourage, cajole or convince others to garner commitment to their mission. The right story can be the best tool. Rather than arguing along the lines of "you should do this because," you can tell a story that makes the same point but also engages the hearts of your listeners. Outstanding leaders like Steve Case of AOL have used strategic stories well. The war story from the beginning of this chapter about his meeting with Bill Gates was just one strategic tool Case used skillfully to mobilize his company against Microsoft.

To make a point about integrity, saying "You must keep your word" or "We ought to walk our talk" does not inspire anyone. Instead, tell a strategic story that conveys integrity. When I recently wanted to persuade a senior manager to focus personally on business development, I told him how Churchill voluntarily went into the trenches during World War I in order to do himself what he had asked others to do as First Lord of the Admiralty. (Later, when Churchill reminded Field Marshall Montgomery that he needed to be less aloof from his troops and venture out into the front lines, the Field Marshall replied with the adage that "familiarity breeds contempt." Churchill shot back: "My friend, familiarity breeds a lot of other things, too...") Perhaps my little story gave the manager a context for his actions and a new way of looking at his work on the front lines.

> **Tip.** Become a strategic storyteller. Gather vignettes and war stories about leadership and accomplishments in history and in your own life, and use them to inspire people.

Open Secret #6: Humor. The final secret of productive speaking is humor. The comedian and business consultant Steve Rizzo maintains that business people underestimate the power of humor. Humor is essential to emotional stability, says Rizzo: "Humor can nip negative thoughts in the bud."

The final secret of productive speaking is humor. Business people underestimate the power of humor.

For centuries, minorities and oppressed people with no weapons other than their wit have used humor strategically to outsmart their oppressors. The Brazilian rabbi Nilton Bonder tells a story of a Jew in medieval times who was imprisoned without trial by an evil ruler. As a way to decide the prisoner's fate, the ruler handed him a bag that he said contained two balls, one black and one white. The prisoner was told to take one ball out without looking. If he chose the white ball, he would be freed; but if he chose the black one, he would be executed. The prisoner knew immediately that his captors had put two black balls in the bag. How could he save himself from certain death? In a flash of intuition, he scooped a ball out of the bag and swallowed it so quickly that no one could see its color. His captors said, "What are you doing? Now we don't know which ball you have chosen." The prisoner answered, "No problem. Just see which ball is still in the bag." He had beaten his captors with his quick wit.

The comedian and civil rights leader Dick Gregory demonstrated the power of humor against overwhelming physical force. On April 2, 1963, Gregory participated in black voter registration marches in Greenwood, Mississippi. When the mayor in a public speech solemnly enumerated the character deficiencies that made blacks unqualified to vote, Gregory stepped forward with a beaming smile: "Well, now, Mr. Mayor. You really took your nigger pills last night, didn't you?" Gregory's banter had a powerful effect on the crowd, who saw that the dominion of whites was in place

> Humor can empower your people by making a challenge easier to tackle, helping them work together to achieve a common goal, or disarming tension and minimizing adversity.

merely because they had accepted it for so long. That night, Gregory gave a short and passionate speech. "We will march through your dogs!" he cried. "And if you get some elephants, we'll march through them. And bring on your tigers and we'll march through them!" As people laughed, their tension and fear melted away.[53]

Of course humor is not always productive. As Sigmund Freud observed, jokes can be thinly veiled weapons of aggression. But humor can empower your people by making a challenge easier to tackle, helping them work together to achieve a common goal, or disarming tension and minimizing adversity.

Rizzo, the comedian, gives four tips for keeping humor present in life:

1. Each day, find something to laugh at. If you can't find something, look in the mirror.

2. When in traffic, look at others as if they were circus performers.

3. Remember that you have the right to enjoy yourself.

4. Find the humor in the very stuff that upsets you. Humor is more powerful than anger. (That, however, is easier said than done. Rizzo admits: "Whether you practice it or not is a different question.")

But be sure to hit the sense of humor that is right for your listeners. This can be difficult in cross-cultural settings where your jokes are easily misunderstood (or send people straight to sleep, as happened to me in Japan). You will do this right if you stand in the shoes of your listeners.

Disclaimers

As we come to the end of the book, two disclaimers are in order. First, communication is not always the necessary ingredient. I know companies where people are terrible at communicating, but their product is so good that they simply don't have to. The product speaks for itself, and customers buy it. In one software company the R&D division steadfastly refuses to report to headquarters. Headquarters calls them "the cowboys"—except that the cowboys keep producing the most valuable new ideas. Their innovation surpasses that of all other divisions that report like clockwork.

Communication cannot ultimately be institutionalized or legislated.

Second, full communication is, of course, not the only success factor. We learn from failed CEOs that communication problems are not always the primary cause of their failure. It can be bad earnings news (as with Frank Lorenzo at Continental). It can be decision gridlock (as was the case with Robert Allen at AT&T). It can be that the CEO is simply missing in action (as with John Sculley at Apple). But a 1999 survey of 93 failed CEOs by *Fortune* magazine showed that a third of them had problems that could have been solved with good communication. Another third had bad earnings news, and you could make a case that the question is how you communicate bad news. Above all, don't do it like Jill Barad of Mattel, who announced twice in one year that there was no problem with performance, only to surprise shareholders within weeks with bad news that eroded her credibility and sent stocks tumbling.

A last point is that communication cannot ultimately be institutionalized or legislated. It is an intention, not a structure. People need to have an inherent desire to communicate to others. Don't confuse a communication structure with communication. Communication should never be an end in itself. It is a means to an end. If people can produce the result without communicating, by all means, let them. But be mindful of the potential pitfalls: if communication is top-down or lacking altogether, you are unlikely to have innovation. As my old friend, the Australian entrepreneur Rob Turnbull summed it up once: "Tell people the breakdowns. Be public. The biggest failure is not to communicate."[54]

Tip. Observe the patterns of speech around you. Does a statement point to the past, rob people of their power or put a damaging spin on things? Or does it point to the future and open new vistas? Experiment with the Open Secrets of productive speaking.

The Bottom Line

- Leadership and communication are intertwined. To be a great leader, you must be a great communicator.

- Language has the power to shape reality. That is both the good and the bad news.

- From post-merger pains to employee burnout or departmental warfare, there is hardly an issue that cannot be settled through complete communication. But we fail to take advantage of this exquisite medium. Much of what we say—including rumors, judgments, excuses and threats—is careless or unproductive.

- Listening is not a soft skill. Lack of listening has hard consequences, from opportunity costs to merger pains, from employee burnout to lawsuits. Effective listening leads to tangible results. But listening is underrated and under-researched as a leadership tool.

- Listening is not like a light switch that you turn on and off. Seven levels of listening range from ignoring someone all the way to generating the speaker's brilliance. The highest skill of communication is the ability to hear how others are listening to you, which enables you to speak to their listening.

- Yes, there are times when listening is wrong because it makes room for dangerous ideas or disingenuous talk. But most of us err in the opposite direction: we don't listen enough.

- If you ask a question that requires a "yes or no" answer, don't accept any other answer than "yes" or "no." People tend to give you all kinds of information you didn't ask for. Stop them politely and tell them you want a simple "yes" or "no."

- We could vastly improve our effectiveness by communicating rigorously and productively—with declarations, commitments, requests, invitations, stories and humor.

- Leaders lead by making outlandish promises and requests.

Appendix One

Troubleshooting Manual

Be patient towards all that is unresolved in your life,
and try to love the questions themselves.
Do not now seek the answers which cannot be given to you
because you would not be able to live them,
and the point is to live everything.
Live the questions now. Perhaps you will then,
gradually, without noticing it,
live some long distant day into the answers.

Rainer Maria Rilke

Leaders are, by definition, troubleshooters. Without troubles, there is no need for leaders. This book is designed as a reference guide that leaders can consult time and again in their ongoing quest for excellence; this appendix deals with some of the problems that may arise for leaders in the heat of the action. It took Moses, perhaps the greatest leader in human history, reportedly took forty years to lead his people out of Egypt. His path was not likely strewn with roses. Ever since Moses, paths of leaders have been fraught with setbacks. Like Moses, emerging leaders will feel lost in their own desert of trials and tribulations. This Troubleshooting Manual offers solutions to simple questions, such as: "What do I do if the waters of the Red Sea do not part at my command? What if the burning bush does not talk to me, or if it does talk but my people fail to believe that the bush talked?"

Of course it is impossible to foresee, let alone cover, all the possible troubles that might be candidates for troubleshooting. However, readers might find enough ideas and cross-references here to put together their own strategies and tactics for dealing with the inevitable obstacles along the way. And remember: obstacles are the very stuff of which leadership is fashioned. Without obstacles, there is no leadership—life would be boring. Without leadership, there are no obstacles—but also no adventure, no vitality, no growth, no fun.

At the outset, one piece of advice may be relevant to many of the situations that follow—so relevant indeed that it is a nearly universal solution to problems involving other people. When you see a problem in your organization or people, instead of looking for a solution outside yourselves, you do well to first look inside. Is it possible that the behavior you spurn in others is one that you exhibit yourself, but fail to recognize? For example, if you blame others for not listening, might it be that you are the one whose ears are closed off? If you complain about rumors, are you yourself talking about others irresponsibly? If no one follows through on the details, could it be that you are not letting them take charge?

One benefit (for better or for worse) of relating closely with other people is that others mirror our flaws for us. It is a commonplace that whatever we cannot abide in others is an aspect of our own personality that we fail to see. Rather than seeing others as an irritant, we can hold the people with whom we live and work as guideposts pointing us to the characteristics and behaviors that we are ready to transform in ourselves so as to be more effective leaders.

Tip. Remember that you cannot change others—the only person you can change, if at all, is yourself. Make it a practice to look to yourself first when you see a problem in others. This practice will not solve all problems; after all, some issues are simply there—you did nothing to create them. Looking first to yourself may or may not be the ultimate solution. But it is always the appropriate place to begin.

There is another aspect of looking to ourselves first: leadership happens by example. It is essential that we model the characteristics and behaviors we want to see in others. If we want others to be egoless, we need to put our own egos aside. If we want others to take risks, we need to transcend our own caution and desire to play it safe. If we want others to keep their agreements, we need to be meticulous in keeping our own. We need to walk our talk. We cannot ask others to go where we will not venture.

What to Do When...

A war is on in your organization. A few years ago, the basketball player Latrell Sprewell snapped and went for the neck of his boss. He throttled the shorter and less well-muscled coach of the Golden State Warriors, threatened to kill him, departed to cool off, did not cool off, returned, and delivered a blow to the senior officer.

It did not have to come to this. Before strangling a truculent boss, there are several strategies you can muster before wrapping your fingers around the offending windpipe:

1. You can discuss cordially that there must have been a misunderstanding, and that the boss believes he has told you something when in fact he did not. Tell the boss calmly: "I am sorry if there is a misunderstanding between us. Let me tell you what you really said, which—now this is kind of funny—was just about the opposite of what you just told me you think you said."

2. You can appeal to the boss's humanity. Refuse to get worked up. Never react emotionally to an accusation. Tell the boss in an amicable way that you don't appreciate being yelled at. Remember, talk about your experience of the boss's words, rather than characterizing the boss in any way. For example: "I want to do better, too, but when you say X, my experience is that I feel unjustly accused, and it's hard for me to improve when I feel so bad about myself."

3. You can talk to your boss's superior. For example, "I have nothing against this guy, he is a terrific coach, but he is really down on me lately. Do you see another way of dealing with his anger?"

4. You can simply say nothing. Refuse to take part. Walk out the door, or make conversation with your peers. And be sure that the problem with your boss does not affect your performance. Show the boss that you are focused on the results and are out there doing the best for the company every day.

5. You can issue a warning. "Stop getting on my case. I am warning you."

6. And if all that has no effect, you can choke him. You will get fired, but maybe the job was not worth it after all.[55]

Communication is absent or insufficient. It is always important to look at yourself first. Are you listening? Are you enhancing open communication? If you focus more on listening to the other person than on being listened to, that might handle a good part of the issue. Leading by example can be very important.

If others do not respond, however, you may need to be more direct—to say, "please don't interrupt me" or "I don't mean to antagonize you, but I don't experience that you're listening to me" or "I don't think you heard what he said." Always listen to the other person, but when your own example is not sufficient, demand that people listen to you and to one another.

Another way of leading by example is to repeat back to the other person what she said to you. "Ah—I see what you're saying," you might say, "you said XYZ." Such repetition may sound somewhat mechanistic at first, but hearing what another person says is so rare that repeating can be a very effective demonstration that you are indeed listening.

A word about the speaking part of communication: if people are saying only the tip of the iceberg of what they really think, be as honest and open as possible, and encourage others to be honest with you. In conversations, ask, "Is there anything else?" When people do communicate with you, keep an open mind. Do not use what they say against them or against anyone else. Demonstrate that they can tell you anything without "pushing your buttons." In short, create a climate of honesty, truthfulness and straightforward talk.

Rumors and gossip distract people from performing. Rumors or gossip are never aimed directly at their targets. People say things about others who are not there—often in a way that produces no results, only agreement. Rumors and gossip can be the single most damaging behavior in organizations. At the very least, they distract people from producing results.

If you are in a position of authority, outlaw rumors. Make it a staff agreement that there be no rumors. This means that if someone on your staff has a problem, that person agrees to speak about it only to someone who can do something about that problem—and not to anyone else. If people break this agreement, they should be warned, or in extreme cases fired. Punishing people for spreading rumors does your organization a great service.

If you are not in a position of sufficient authority, first of all, do not participate in rumors. If people gossip in your presence, let them know that you would rather not participate. If the gossip is in the form of a complaint, suggest that they take the complaint to someone who can do something about it. If you are someone who can do something about the complaint, by all means help resolve it. Do not allow rumors to fester. Recommend to those in authority that they institute a policy that forbids rumors.

Bickering or belligerence are rampant. Bickering is similar to spreading rumors, only more overt. Petty squabbling can include passive-aggressive behavior, such as putting people down, making jokes about them, or otherwise discounting their statements . Belligerence is similar to bickering, only less petty. Both behaviors provoke animosity.

If you are in a position of authority, arrest bickering or belligerence in your organization. Encourage straight talk without accusations, threats or ultimatums. Create a climate in which people can say what they think, believe or feel, without having to clothe their thoughts in caustic, sarcastic or devious allusions. Reprimand people privately if they continue to bicker or act belligerent. Build policies and a culture of honesty in the organization. Have people come directly to you and make it clear that there will be no negative repercussions for honesty. If you hear of people being punished by their immediate superiors for coming to you directly, punish those superiors swiftly. Warn them that continued infractions could cost them their jobs. If the behavior continues, let the person go. People drilling holes in the boat had better get off the boat.

If you are not in a position of authority, take the actions recommended in the previous section.

Perhaps the most effective way of preventing negative talk is to create and maintain a larger context. Keep vision present for people.

Talk is full of justification, explanation and excuses. Justification, explanation, and excuses are all communications that do not produce results but take the place of results. Create a culture that prohibits justifications, explanations and excuses. There is widespread evidence that when people are not able to use these types of communications, they are forced to focus on solutions and accomplishments. Rather than using the majority of their energy—and their working hours—on why something is not happening, they can use that same energy determining what can be done about it, and taking effective action. Refrain from justifying your-self, and do not accept it from others. Have people see the differ-ence it makes to communicate using commitments and requests, instead of excuses for why the results have not happened.

People repeatedly miss key performance targets. When people miss their goals, they often lose confidence or become resigned. (In my own case, all it takes to get discouraged is for three people in a row to say "No" to me.)

When goals or targets are missed, never ignore it. If you ignore lack of performance, you are seen as condoning it. Instead you should stop the action for a moment, call the team together if necessary, debrief the actions taken so that your colleagues can learn from their experience, and permit them to complete their experience so they can move on. If resignation is present, enable team members to recommit to the overall vision, even if it seems far off. Then align on a minimum-acceptable target that shall be met no matter what. Set this target so as to enable people to win. With each win, you can slowly reestablish the confidence people gain from delivering their targets.

People do not keep agreements. This is similar to the problem of people missing their targets. Lack of compliance with agreements cannot be ignored either. When people fail to keep agreements, sit down with them and, if necessary, reestablish why the agree-ment is there in the first place. Give them the background for the agreement again. Have them own the rationale. Ask them to recommit to it. Don't be punitive. At the same time, don't pretend that they did not break the agreement.

Ignoring is one of the worst things you can do in an organiza-tion. When a communication is ignored, it undermines the power of all communications in the organization. It calls into question the credibility of all commitments. If one does not matter, none of them matters. In such a climate, you have no basis on which to operate. If your co-worker says that he needs a report by Friday, ignoring that he said that—perhaps because you are busy—is extremely dis-empowering to him. Let him know that you cannot provide the report by Friday, but that you will by Monday, or tell him what you can do by Friday. Don't ignore what others say. Treat all communication as worthy of your attention.

Tip. Treat all communications as if they were commitments.

Your boss is a dictator. Your boss—or, for that matter, your teacher, your spouse, a political or religious leader—may be an autocrat who makes decisions unilaterally, without informing or consulting people. Independence can be a core value, especially in the United States. Dictators are simply an extreme case of that value. One thing you can do if you have to deal with a dictator is to create a very deep relationship with that person. Dictators tend not to trust anybody. Earning their trust will hopefully create a relationship based on co-creation. If you are your boss's perfect understudy, or the favorite student, or the ideal employee, have him become your mentor. He will probably come to experience some level of trust for you. This means that your voice can be heard, which in turn means that he will make fewer decisions unilaterally.

Another, similar approach is to manage your boss invisibly, seemingly doing what he wants, but actually guiding him and putting the information and displays in front of him that will have him make the right decisions. You want him to act based on the information that you present to him. This again requires a sound relationship with him.

If that does not work, another option is to bypass the dictator by assembling the partnership of other, like-minded colleagues— but be prepared to live with the consequences of such open mutiny. If all else fails, a final option is to throw the rascal out. Try to stage a revolution or a coup, and align everyone on getting rid of the dictator. The danger is that you will fail. The danger of the first approach, by contrast, is that you will sell out and be the dictator's tool. There is no perfect solution; you have to judge the situation for yourself.

Appendix Two

Resources

Our clients often ask if I can suggest tools or resources that could help them communicate more effectively with other people. This section is my response to those requests. If you read these books and incorporate their lessons into your daily interactions, both your results and the quality of your life may improve tangibly. (Then again, they may not.)

Branch, Taylor. 1988. *Parting the Waters: America in the King Years, 1954–63*. New York: Simon & Schuster.

Buber, Martin. 1974. *I and Thou*. New York: Scribner.

Cohen, Don and Laurence Prusak. 2001. *In Good Company: How Social Capital Makes Organizations Work*. Cambridge, MA: Harvard Business School Press.

Flaherty, James. 1999. *Coaching: Evoking Excellence in Others*. Woburn, MA: Butterworth–Heinemann.

Flores, Fernando and Terry Winograd. 1986. *Understanding Computers and Cognition*. Norwood, NJ: Ablex Publishing Corporation.

Goleman, Daniel. 2000. *Working with Emotional Intelligence*. New York: Bantam Books.

Heidegger, Martin. 1971. *On the Way to Language*. San Francisco: Harper & Row.

Kinlaw, Dennis C. 1989. *Coaching for Commitment*. San Diego, CA: University Associates, Inc.

Nichols, Michael P. 1995. *The Lost Art of Listening*. New York: Guilford Publications.

Searle, John R. 1969. *Speech Acts.* Cambridge: Cambridge University Press.

Tannen, Deborah. 1990. *You Just Don't Understand.* New York: Ballantine Books.

Thompson, Peter. 1998. *Persuading Aristotle: The Timeless Art of Persuasion in Business, Negotiation and the Media.* St. Leonards, NSW, Australia: Allen & Unwin.

Endnotes

1 *New York Times,* 7 June 2002, A22.

2 *New York Times,* 2 June 2002, A4.

3 Buber, Martin. 1950. *The Way of Man: According to the Teachings of Hassidism.* London: Routledge and Kegan Paul.

4 *New York Times,* 3 May 1999, A1/A10.

5 Goldin, Hyman. 1962. *Ethics of the Fathers.* New York: Hebrew Publishing Company, 10.

6 *Neue Züercher Zeitung,* 3 January 2001, 33.

7 Rifkin, Jeremy. 1996. *The End of Work: The Decline of the Global Labor Force and the Dawn of the Post-Market Era.* New York: Tarcher/Putnam.

8 Margolis, D.R. 1979. *The Managers: Corporate Life in America.* New York: William Morrow; Ehrensal, Kenneth N. 1995. "Discourses of Global Competition," *Journal of Organizational Change Management,* vol.8, no.5, Fall.

9 Hammer, Michael and James Champy. 2001. *Reengineering the Corporation: A Manifesto for Business Revolution.* New York: Harper Business.

10 From a study that accompanied workers laid off from a shipyard in their first steps as free agents. One former shipyard worker reports that "I did this out of sheer desperation. After all, I had to begin somehow. How old was I? 50, no 51."

11 Mandel, Oscar. *Blossoms and Incantations* (E-Book; self-published).

12 Heidegger, Martin. [1971] 1982. *On the Way to Language.* San Francisco: Harper Row, 57.

13 Rubin, Harriet. "The Power of Words," *Fast Company* 21, January 1999, 142.

[14] *New York Times,* 13 June 2001, H3; 18 August 2000, B11; 5 November 2001, G4; 31 August 2000, G1; 5 July 2000, C1; 1 August 2000, A10; 25 January 2001, G10.

[15] 2000 commencement address, University of Southern Maine, Portland; *New York Times,* 29 May 2000, A11.

[16] *Christian Science Monitor,* 24 May 2000, 1.

[17] 2000 commencement address, University of California at Berkeley; *New York Times,* 29 May 2000, A11.

[18] *Fortune,* 10 July 2000, 114–126.

[19] Tuchman, Barbara. 1971. *Stilwell and the American Experience in China,* 1911–45. New York: Macmillan.

[20] Swisher, Kara. 1998. *aol.com: How Steve Case Beat Bill Gates, Nailed the Netheads, and Made Millions in the War for the Web.* New York: Random House, 160.

[21] Vidal, Gore. 1996. *Palimpsest.* London: Abacus. 387. No wonder a British survey of pet owners has shown that 45 percent of women—almost half—would rather spend time with their animals than with their boyfriend or life partner. "An animal seems to be a great listener," explains Glyn Collis, a psychologist and animal expert. "It does not answer, does not just run away, and stays always patient—not like a man." *Der Spiegel,* 22/2002; translation mine.

[22] Brands, H.W. 1999. *Masters of Enterprise.* New York: Free Press, 296.

[23] Survey by the Coleman Consulting Group, reported in "Hellooo. Anybody Listening?" *Management Review,* vol. 86, issue 10, November 1997.

[24] *New York Times,* 15 November 2000, C1.

[25] Claus, Leigh Ann. 1997. "IBM Canada holds on to its beliefs— and its future," *Quality Progress,* vol. 30, issue 10, October, 37–41.

[26] Rasmusson, Erika. 1997. "Winning back angry customers," *Sales and Marketing Management,* vol. 149, issue 11, October, 131.

[27] Ferris, Roger M. 1997. "PE Interviews: Neil Kadisha," *Plastics Engineering,* December, 20–22.

[28] Nichols, Michael P. 1995. *The Lost Art of Listening: How Listening Can Improve Relationships.* New York: Guilford Press.

[29] Elaine Sciolino, "The People's Shah," *The New York Times Book Review,* 27 August 2000.

[30] *Brands, ibid,* 310–312.

[31] Daniels, Cora. 2000. "How to Goof Off At Your Next Meeting," *Fortune,* October 30, 289.

[32] Laver, Ross. 1998. *Random Excess: The Wild Ride of Michael Cowpland and Corel.* Viking Canada.

[33] David S. Pottruck and Terry Pearce. 2000. *Clicks and Mortar: Passion Driven Growth in an Internet Driven World.* San Francisco: Jossey Bass.

[34] "Postal Service Becomes a Model of Conciliation," *New York Times,* 7 September 2000, C1.

[35] Brands, *ibid,* 791.

[36] Branch, Taylor. 1988. *Parting the Waters: America in the King Years, 1954–63.* New York: Simon & Schuster.

[37] *New York Times,* 8 November 2001, S4.

[38] Brands, *ibid,* 272.

[39] *New York Times,* 12 August 2000, C1.

[40] *New York Times,* 4 August 2002, sec. 3:12.

[41] Brands, *ibid,* 248-249.

[42] Brands, *ibid,* 539.

[43] *Wall Street Journal,* 26 October 2000, B20.

[44] Brands, *ibid,* 318, 321.

[45] Brands, *ibid,* 321.

[46] Swisher, *ibid,* 77–83.

[47] Not everyone agrees. According to evolutionary psychologist Nigel Nicholson, gossip was a skill needed by our Stone Age ancestors to survive the socially unpredictable conditions of the Savannah Plain. Thus, over time, gossip became part of our mental programming. Nicholson argues that executives trying to eradicate gossip at work might as well try to change their employees' musical tastes. (Nigel Nicholson, "How Hardwired Is Human Behavior?" *Harvard Business Review,* July–August 1998, 134–147.) Don Cohen and Laurence Prusak also argue in their book *In Good Company: How Social Capital Makes Organizations Work* that "Telling and listening to stories, chatting, sharing a little gossip, are the main ways that people in organizations come to trust and understand one another." Maybe so, but when people are fearful of being straightforward and honest with one another, when they have to resort to rumor and gossip, the organization is in trouble. Managers should still foster a culture of honesty and straight talk.

[48] Scherr, Allan L. 1989. "Managing for Breakthroughs in Productivity," *Human Resource Management* 28:3 (Fall), 403–424.

[49] Young, H. *et al.* 1970. *Journey to Tranquillity: the History of Man's Assault on the Moon.* New York: Doubleday, 109–110. Cited in Johnson, Paul. 1985. *Modern Times: The World from the Twenties to the Eighties.* New York: Harper & Row, 1985, 630.

[50] Manchester, William. 1988. *Winston Spencer Churchill: The Last Lion; Alone: 1932-1940.* New York: Dell Publishing.

[51] Speech, "The Strenuous Life," 10 April 1899. The Hamilton Club, Chicago.

[52] Brands, *ibid,* 278.

[53] Branch, *ibid,* 722.

[54] Interview, 29 January 2001.

[55] "Bing!" *Fortune,* 12 January 1998, 57–58.

The Author

Thomas D. Zweifel (tdz@swissconsultinggroup.com) is a specialist in building and coaching global high-performance teams. The co-founder and CEO of Swiss Consulting Group (www.swissconsultinggroup.com) has lived on four continents and coached global leaders in Fortune 500 companies and small businesses, government and the military, non-governmental organizations and the UN since 1984. He and his clients achieved breakthrough results in the most diverse cultural environments—and often under adverse circumstances.

Born in Paris, Zweifel holds dual citizenship in Switzerland and the United States, and is fluent in English, German, French and Italian. He holds a Ph.D. in International Relations from New York University and teaches leadership in international and public affairs at Columbia University. Publishing frequently on leadership and democracy, global citizenship and communication, Zweifel is the author of *Democratic Deficit? The European Union, Switzerland, and the United States in Comparative Perspective* (Lexington Books, 2002) and *International Organizations: Democracy, Accountability and Power* (Lynne Rienner, 2003). He lives in New York City.

Your toughest time ever?

When I lived and worked in India, I almost died of a double infection—bacterial and amoebic at the same time. The doctor came and said: "You must go to the hospital." I said: "No, I have no time for this, I have work to do." He simply slapped me in the face and took me to Bombay Hospital. I was in a room with eight others, and all the religions of the world were represented in the room— Hindus and Buddhists and Catholics and Muslims, and there was wailing and praying night and day. A nurse sat next to my bed for nine days and nine nights. Along with losing almost all the water in my body, I hopefully lost some arrogance and gained some humility.

It took seven years to install a phone line while I lived in India. My task was to train fourteen local leaders to deliver a workshop across the nation. My efforts were frustrated at every turn. It was very, very hard, but I got the job done. As a consequence of our effort, millions of people have taken charge of their destiny and have uplifted themselves from the conditions of hunger.

Your worst job ever?

Once I was consulting an organization where no one listened to each other. It was almost physically painful to even be there. When people don't listen to each other, they jeopardize organizations.

Your greatest concern about the future?

Consumerism. My greatest fear is that we become passive, resigned, indifferent, self-centered individuals who have no interest in serving the community.

Your heroes?

Two leaders: Churchill, for embodying leadership and for reminding us that "We make a living by what we get, but we make a life by what we give." And Gandhi, whom Churchill called "that little naked man," for teaching us integrity. My favorite story about Gandhi is this:

Once, a mother traveled for many days—by train, by rickshaw, by bus and by foot—to bring her young son to Mahatma Gandhi. She begged, "Please, Mahatma. Tell my son to stop eating sugar."

Gandhi was silent for a moment. He said, "Bring your son back in two weeks." The woman was puzzled, but she thanked him and said that she would do as he had asked. She traveled all the way back to her village.

Two weeks later, she undertook the entire trip again—train, rickshaw, bus and foot—and returned with her son. When they stood before Gandhi again, he looked the youngster in the eye and said, "Stop eating sugar."

Grateful but bewildered, the woman asked, "Why did you tell me to bring him back in two weeks? You could have told him the same thing then."

Gandhi replied, "Two weeks ago, *I* was eating sugar."

Also by Thomas D. Zweifel...

- *Culture Clash: Managing the Global High-Performance Team.* 2002. New York: SelectBooks/Swiss Consulting Group.
- *Democratic Deficit? The European Union, Switzerland, and the United States in Comparative Perspective.* 2002. Lanham, MD: Lexington Books/Rowman & Littlefield.

Forthcoming...

- *Coaching Leaders: How to Unleash People Power and Performance.* 2003. New York: Swiss Consulting Group.
- *Strategy-in-Action: People-Centered Strategy that Gets Results.* 2003. With Tapas K. Sen Ph.D. New York: Swiss Consulting Group.
- *International Organizations: Democracy, Accountability and Power.* 2003. Boulder, CO: Lynne Rienner Publishers.

Go to www.swissconsultinggroup.com to find out more and/or to join Swiss Consulting Group's mailing list. If you found any inaccuracies in this book, we would be grateful if you told us. Send an email to books@swissconsultinggroup.com or call us at 212-288-4858.

Cognitive Styles:

       Open-minded vs. closed-minded

Process   Associative vs Abstractive.
ing.

Behavior and   Particular   vs   Universal
thinking.

    Negotiation Strategies

What is the truth.

       Faith, Fact or Feeling

Grupo afortunado — responsabilidad

   no. valores ofida — identes

   etica — social responsibilitves

Priviledge